Happy Thoughts for Bad Hair Days

Happy Thoughts for Bad Hair Days

Andrea Stephens

Vine Books
Servant Publications
Ann Arbor, Michigan

Vine Books is an imprint of Servant Publications especially designed to serve evangelical Christians.

Published by Servant Publications
P.O. Box 8617
Ann Arbor, Michigan 48107

Cover design: PAZ Design Group-Salem, Oregon

01 02 03 04 10 9 8 7 6 5 4 3 2 1

Printed in the United States of America
ISBN 1-56955-239-8

Library of Congress Cataloging-in-Publication Data

Stephens, Andrea.
Happy Thoughts for Bad Hair Days / Andrea Stephens.
p. cm.
ISBN 1-56955-239-8 (alk. paper)
1. Teenage girls—Prayer-books and devotions—English. I. Title.

BV4860 .S735 2001
242'.633—dc21

2001035517

Dedication

To Francie George—
You've blessed my life
with your ability to patiently listen
as I pour out my thoughts
on both good and bad hair days!
Everyone needs a friend like you!

Contents

Intro Chat With Andrea!

Some days it looks great. You know, totally cool. It parts just right, it curls just right, and it's not overly frizzy.

Then there are the other 363 days of the year!

You mousse. You gel. You defuse. You spray. You spritz. And it's *still* doing its own thing. The WRONG thing!

It's out of control.

It's unbearable!

It's unwearable!

It's your ... HAIR!

Everybody's got it and some days it can be hard to deal with. No matter how much effort you put into it, it adds up to one thing ... A BAD HAIR DAY.

Last summer, I spent a week at the beach with my relatives. One day I had been out in the waves trying my skill on the boogie board (stomach surfing, I call it). I thought I was dazzling in my execution of the boogie board until I found out I was supposed to catch a wave and *ride* the thing, not just paddle around on it!

Anyway, after being washed up on the sand like a beached whale, I decided enough was enough. So I headed toward our beach umbrella, then toweled off and slipped on my cover-up and sun visor. Now if you've ever been to the beach, you know it is not unusual for the wind to be whipping around. Well, it *whipped* all right. Sand was swirling everywhere and so was my hair! It was more than I could take, so I headed back to our condo.

Upon arriving, my seven-year-old niece took one look at me and squeaked out, "Bad hair day, Aunt Annie?" Ornery girl. I chased her down and tickled her for teasing me.

Then I looked in the mirror.

"Bad" was putting it nicely! Disastrous was more like it! My half-dry, wind-whipped, naturally curly hair was everywhere! The pieces hanging over the front of my visor were especially attractive!

We have all had crummy hair days. And we'll all have more!

They are bound to happen! Unstoppable! Unpredictable! Inevitable! But they don't have to rock our confidence.

They don't have to make us feel completely self-conscious all day.

They don't have to ruin our mood or rule our emotions!

There are lots of other things that have the potential to do that!

Just like our hairstyles, some of our days are good, some bad. Some are great, while others crash and burn (or at least it feels that way).

Maybe yesterday things were going perfectly—you looked great, you passed your history exam, that cute new guy said hi to you.

But today? Hair? Zero! Calculus quiz? Flunked! Cafeteria? Ran out of pizza again! PMS? Oh, yeah!

See, there are days where externally your hair is lookin' fine but internally things are not looking so good. Yes! There are *external* bad hair days and *internal* bad hair days!

But wait. Here's some good news!

You don't have to allow the details of your day to determine your outlook, mash your mood, or burst your confidence bubble.

In fact, every day can be a good day. Even if you start out in a funk, you can end up feeling fantastic!

It all starts with your thoughts.

Yep, that beautiful brain of yours is a powerful tool!

Happy thoughts can cure bad hair days—the external ones *and* the internal ones.

How does it work?

It is easier than you think. It's all about putting a lid on the negative thoughts and letting the positive ones soar! Yep, choose to see the positive side of things.

How?

First, look to God's Word. There you will find words of inspiration. The wisest thing you can ever learn to do in any situation is to go to the Bible and see what God has to say. It's true! His Word can boost your mood and elevate your thoughts above the ho-hum, doldrums, frustrations, stresses, ouches, pitfalls, and nasties of everyday life.

You can rise above the impossible when you look to the Lord.

Besides, where else is there to go?

When David says in Psalm 121 that he lifted up his eyes to the hills, it means he looked up toward heaven. That is where his help came from. And when he was weary, he asked God and *God* lifted his head so he could look toward heaven (see Psalm 3:3). Focus on God. Read the Word. Redirect your thoughts. Line them up with the Scriptures. They are the source of your encouragement!

Second, learn to be grateful. Counting your blessings and looking for things to be grateful for—no matter how grave the situation or how gross your hair looks—will brighten the dullest of days. It will help you grow to appreciate yourself, your family, your friends, your teachers, your coaches, and your LIFE!

In the following pages you will discover happy thoughts for both kinds of bad hair days—external and internal. You will find encouraging words, inspiring thoughts, helpful hints, and tons of advice. We will chat about happy thoughts for bad hair days, fickle friendship days, super moody days, and rough family days.

My prayer is that as you fix your mind on these happy thoughts and as you allow them to sink into your heart, they will lead to happy days ... no matter *what* your hair looks like! We're in this together!

Andrea

~ Section One ~

HAPPY THOUGHTS FOR BAD HAIR DAYS!

Whatever is true, whatever is noble, whatever is right,

whatever is pure, whatever is lovely,

whatever is admirable —

if anything is excellent or praiseworthy —

think about such things!

Philippians 4:8 (NIV)

Someone Cares About Your 'Do More Than You!

Fifty-one, fifty-two, fifty-three, fifty-four, fifty—, oh, rats, I lost count! Have you ever tried to count each and every strand of hair on your head? Sounds impossible, huh? Well, it's not for God! He keeps track of your hair. Why is that?

Maybe he can't believe all the hair we leave lying on the bathroom floor! Maybe there's only so much hair to go around, so he has to ration it out. Could be! But probably not. I'll bet he keeps count to emphasize the fact that he never forgets about us. Each day we lose fifty to eighty strands of hair. That sounds like a lot, but nevertheless, the Lord knows exactly how many hairs we have at every moment. Incredible! He knows even the most minor details about us. Think about it. If you lost forty-seven hairs today, would you know it? I'm not sure I would. Yet God does. His concern over our lives proves we are very valuable to him. *We matter to God in a very special way.* His eyes and heart are turned continuously toward us. What can our response to this kind of love be?

An honest effort to be our best and look our best for him is a good start. As children of God we represent him. Our actions and our appearance speak louder than words. We have the privilege to style our hair, groom our appearance, choose modest clothes, and bubble over with beautiful attitudes that honor our heavenly Father. After all, he deserves it! He is the One who cares about every detail of our lives—even our hair.

Are not five sparrows sold for two cents?
And yet not one of them is forgotten before God.
Indeed, the very hairs of your head are all numbered.
Do not fear; you are of more value than many sparrows.
Luke 12: 6-7 (NASB)

HAPPY HINT

Focus your thoughts on the beauty of the Lord
and your hair will hardly even matter!

So, Whatz Hair Anyway?

HAIR \' ha (a)r. \ technically speaking …

~ A slender threadlike outgrowth of the epidermis (top layer of skin) primarily on the scalp! (Though it appears on various other body parts!)

~ Composed of a strong protein called keratin which has twenty-one different amino acids.

~ Each hair strand or shaft consists of three parts:

<u>The cuticle:</u> the outer layer which is made of tiny scalelike cells that point downward, overlapping each other and protecting the inner layers.
<u>The cortex:</u> the middle layer which is a fibrous substance with long cells, designed to give elasticity and strength to the hair; also contains the pigment that gives hair its color.
<u>The medulla:</u> the core or center that determines hair thickness.

SYNONYMS \ also known as …Tresses, locks, mane, mop!
HAIRDO \' ha(a)r-. dü \
~ A way of dressing or wearing the hair; style, coiffure, 'do, (or some days just "do-do").

HAPPY THOUGHT

Don't like your 'do?

Wash it, dry it,

and do it again!

Unplug Your Powerful Hair!

Hair is pretty wimpy. It has no muscles. No vocal cords. No ability to stand up and push you around. Yet how many times have you allowed your hair to make you feel unattractive? How many days have you wanted to pull the sheets up over your head and stay in bed after one look at your tresses? How many birthday bashes or football games or youth group gatherings have you decided to ditch because you felt your hair didn't look right?

If you have done *any* of these things, then you have allowed your wimpy, muscle-less, voiceless hair to pack a power punch. You have empowered your hair! Amazing, isn't it? When you really think about it, it is more than amazing, it is ridiculous. Silly! Perhaps even borderline idiotic!

Only you can unplug the power! Only you can flip the switch and render your hair harmless. When your hair threatens to control you, you have a decision to make. Will you let it affect you? Or, will you fight back by refusing to let it rule your feelings and ruin your social life? Please, unplug! Then choose to jump into your day and put your energies into living free from the stresses of your tresses. After all, there are so many wonderful, worthwhile, winsome things to be influenced by. Your hair is not one of them!

HAPPY HINT

There is a place you can go 24/7 for some awesome encouragement. It's the Bible! Open it up. It always has something wonderful to say.

Shh! God Is Whispering to You . . .

A mother wishing to encourage her young son's progress at the piano bought tickets to a Paderewski performance. When the evening arrived, they found their seats near the front of the concert hall and eyed the majestic Steinway waiting on stage. Soon the mother found a friend to talk to, and the boy slipped away. At eight o'clock, the lights in the auditorium began to dim. The spotlights came on, and only then did they notice the boy … up on the bench, innocently picking out "Twinkle, Twinkle, Little Star."

His mother gasped ... but before she could retrieve her son, the master appeared on the stage and quickly moved to the keyboard. He whispered to the boy, "Don't quit—keep playing." Leaning over, Paderewski reached down with his left hand and began filling in the bass part. Soon his right arm reached around the other side, improvising a delightful obligato. Together, the old master and the young novice held the crowd mesmerized.

In our lives, unpolished though they may be, it is The Master who surrounds us and whispers in our ear time and again, "Don't quit—keep playing." And as we do, he augments and supplements until a work of amazing beauty is created.

Shared by E-mail

HAPPY HINT

Refuse to let a hectic schedule steal your personal time with your heavenly Father! Start each day with God and your life will be more peaceful!

JUST A THOUGHT

Thoughts become Attitudes

Attitudes shape Actions

Actions become Habits

Habits form Character

Character effects Destiny

It all starts with a thought!

Choose to make it a happy one!

Your Hair Is Lovable!

Wavy. Straight. Thin. Thick. Flat. Fluffy. Curly. Frizzy. Whatever your hair's natural condition, you ***can*** grow to love it!

How? By accepting your hair the way God made it! Ouch! Some girls do not want to hear that. Instead, they spend precious time and money trying to get their hair to do something it wasn't designed to do. You know, sort of like the square peg in a round hole thing. It doesn't fit. It doesn't work. And you end up in a royal rage or a frustrated frump! Instead, step back and take inventory.

Describe your hair:

TEXTURE:	____ fine	____ medium	____ coarse
DENSITY:	____ thin	____ medium	____ thick
FORM:	____ straight	____ wavy	____ curly
CONDITION:	____ dry	____ normal	____ oily

Based on your description, ask yourself, "Is my hair actually capable of achieving the style I think I want?"

See, you can try, but you cannot really force your hair to *do* something it can't or *be* something that it's not! For instance, coarse, curly hair will have a hard time wearing a straight, sleek style. Unrealistic expectations about your hair (or about life) will set you up for disappointment!

What's a girl to do?

Accept it. Learn to love it. You will be happier with the results if you select styles that will work with your hair type. So, go ahead. Gently stroke it. Run your fingers through it. Twist it around your finger and give it a little squeeze! Let your hair know you love it just the way it is!

HAPPY HINT

Upper lip hair can be bleached, waxed, or lasered away. Goodbye, moustache!

~ Notable Quotable ~

No one has the right to look with contempt on himself when God has shown such an interest in him.

—Unknown

He Knows Your Name

Have you heard that God knows you by name? How cool to know that when we get to heaven we won't need an ID bracelet with a bunch of numbers on it so that God will know who we are!

He already knows. You are not a number. You are not anonymous. You are not just a girl-at-large. You are a precious member of the family of God, known by your Father!

Think about that for a while.

Doesn't it make you feel good?

Knowing this can make every day a happy day!

I have called you by name; you are mine.
Isaiah 43:1 (LB)

JUST A THOUGHT

No one does everything perfectly the first time they try it!
Don't quit if you did not do something well!
You know the sayings ...
If at first you don't succeed try, try again!
~ and ~
Practice makes perfect!

How to Have Happy Hair!

Give your hair a happy day by taking good care of it! Here are three tress-thrilling tips to put your mane on the road to happiness!

- Shampoo, shampoo, shampoo! This is the first and most vital step in caring for your hair! Choose a pH-balanced product that matches your hair condition (dry, normal, or oily) and texture (fine, medium, or coarse). Rub a quarter-sized squirt of shampoo between your palms. Then apply it evenly to your wet hair. Work the shampoo all the way to the roots, giving an extra scrub at your hairline and the nape of your neck.
- Avoid a too-soft, too-tame, too-greasy look by applying only a tad of conditioner to the ends of your hair. This will help with tangles, too. Be sure to rinse both shampoo and conditioner thoroughly.
- Keep your hair trimmed (every six to eight weeks) to maintain your hairstyle and avoid split ends. You see, when the outer layer of the hair strand is worn away by hot rollers, curling irons, blow dryers, and the like, you will get split ends! Overprocessing hair with

perms and highlights doesn't help, either. Overprocessing steals the natural bounce and shine from healthy hair!

Adapted from
God Thinks You're Positively Awesome,
Servant Publications, 1997

Captivating Thoughts

It is sort of like a daydream. Just sitting and thinking, letting thoughts flow through your mind. Maybe they are thoughts influenced by a TV show, a movie, a magazine article, or a conversation. Some of those thoughts capture our attention. They have an irresistible appeal.

Thoughts can get carried away if we let them run wild. Whether we want to admit it or not, some of what we let roll around in our mind needs to be chased down and captured!

That's correct! If thoughts are not happy or honorable, catch 'em! Read them their rights, cuff 'em, take them into custody, and lock 'em into a cold cell. Yep! Arrest all negative, revengeful, lustful, dishonest, unholy, and self-incriminating thoughts. Then press charges and let the trial begin.

Any thought that says the opposite of God's Word needs to stand trial. For instance ...

Thought	Verdict
I will get her back for this. She will pay.	*Lock it up!*
I have to be in by midnight. My parents are losers.	*Arrest it!*

If I'm careful, I can cheat on this test.	*Put it behind bars!*
What it would feel like to have him touch me?	*Handcuff it!*
I can't finish this project. I'm not smart enough.	*Throw the book at it!*

These thoughts are headed in the wrong direction! If allowed to run wild, they will take you where God does not want you to go. Instead, *they* need to go! In fact, any thought that could potentially become an obstacle in your relationship with Christ or your relationship with others—needs to go! Any thought that could potentially mess up or stop God's plan—needs to go! Any thought that could potentially keep you from becoming everything God has destined for you to become—needs to go! Here's how …

Replace the negative or nasty thought with a positively nice one; one that is in line with God's Word. It is something you will have to *choose* to do.

For instance, replace "I will get her back for this. She will pay" with "I will choose to forgive her and be her friend because God asks me to."

You are the one who has to catch the thought and take it captive. It can be hard, but remember you have the Holy Spirit inside of you to supply the self-control to do it! (He will also help you choose to stop watching or reading stuff that influences you in a negative way.)

After these thoughts are locked up, don't let them out. Throw away the key! No visiting allowed. Now, you are free to think all the *positive, loving, warm, pure, and kind thoughts* that you want.

We demolish arguments and every pretension that sets itself up against the knowledge of God, and we take captive every thought to make it obedient to Christ.
2 Corinthians 10:5 (NIV)

She's All That? Well, Look at You!

In a recent telephone poll conducted by *People* magazine, one thousand women were asked personal questions about their thoughts and feelings on a personal issue ... their BODIES!

It is reported that 80 percent of the women who responded said, "images of women on TV and in movies, fashion magazines and advertising, make them feel insecure about their looks."

It is pretty obvious that if we compare ourselves to the actresses, singers, and models that are made to look trim, toned, and totally perfect, chances are we will end up in the dumps! Comparing causes us to be self-critical and undeniably unsatisfied.

That must be so frustrating for God!

I believe he wants to holler out, "STOP SEARCHING FOR THE PERFECT BODY! YOU ALREADY HAVE IT!"

See, God's perspective on our bodies is very different from Hollywood's. First of all, God has created us in *his* image. He chose this form of body for us! (see Genesis 1:26-27) Second, God designed each of our bodies when he knit us together while we were inside our mother's womb (see Psalm 139). He determined our height, hair color, hip width, breast size, skin tone, and nose shape!

And guess what?

It just so happens that he is quite proud—tickled pink, in fact—with his choices!

The God of the Universe, the creator of the glorious heavens and the incredible earth, the one who created stars and strawberries, snowflakes and snapdragons, did not, I repeat, did not, BLOW IT when he put your body together!

So, get in front of the mirror and take a good look. *You are beautifully created!*

Stop comparing yourself to an airbrushed babe! Those computer retouched gals are not "all that!" You are!

HAPPY HINT

Want to try a new hair color?
First, test the shade by using a tinted mousse
(Sally Beauty Supply) or by trying on a wig in that shade.
Then go with a wash in/wash out color before you make
anything permanent!

~ Notable Quotable ~

UBU! There is no better person to be!
To try to be anything else would be to sell yourself short.
Accept your appearance! Embrace your uniqueness!
Only U can B U!

—Carey Grange, Creator, UBU Cosmetics

A POINT TO PONDER

If you choose to allow Hollywood, TV, magazines, movie stars, or entertainers to influence your opinion of what is beautiful, acceptable, and valuable, you will always be unhappy.

Big Sis Insight: Purposefully Pretty

I would love to have a different nose; I even used to think that it would be great if I got in a little accident—just bad enough that I only had to have a nose job. I'd even dream of the different types of noses I could choose from—I even thought Barbra Streisand's nose was kinda cool! But ultimately I would never do elective nose surgery because this was the beautiful nose that my Maker chose to give me. If I change it I feel I would in effect be saying, "God, you didn't do this right so I'm just going to give you a little help." Today, I thank God for my nose!

God created me just the way he wanted me to be. God has very special and unique plans just for me. And ... that includes MY NOSE. My nose is all part of the wonderful, abundant life that God has planned for me. Looking back often gives me a clearer picture. I was a nice, kind, good girl in high school. NO, I wasn't the prettiest, so I didn't ever date that really cute guy in my English class. I can honestly thank God today for my nose because it kept me out of some potentially difficult situations. I didn't date guys that were interested in me only for looks; I dated some guys that were really neat people who liked me for exactly who I was—nice, kind, and good. Five years after high school, I married one of those guys. Today, after seventeen years of happy marriage to my best friend (who happens to still be very cute), I am very thankful for my God-given nose ... it led me away from danger, and into the arms of a man who loves me the way God loves me.

The Bible says that all things (including my nose) work together for good! It takes time to understand this, but it is so true.

- Ginnie, 39

Permanent Presence!

When a bunch of bad days are all bundled up together and they are threatening to get the best of you, beware! Sometimes it might cause your spiritual life to suffer!

See, you might find yourself asking:

God, where are you?

Don't you know I can't handle this alone?

Why is this happening to me?

You might even find yourself avoiding your prayer time, skipping your devo's, and tuning out during church.

Asking questions during tough times is pretty normal, but watch out! Don't let the enemy use bad hair days to make you doubt God's presence in your life.

When you are doubting that God is really there, you are tempted to turn away from him rather than to him. Turning away is not the answer! You are only delaying your troubles by unplugging yourself from the one Source that can calm your fears and guide you through every bad day in life. You will find the strength, comfort, and direction that you need when you dive toward God, not drop away from him.

If you feel God has rejected you or abandoned you, forcing you to "go it alone" through the tough times of life, you are wrong. He has promised in his Word to never leave you or forsake you. If God seems far away, stop and ask yourself, "Has God moved away or have I?"

James 4:8 assures you that when you draw near to God, he will draw near to you! Perhaps without really realizing, you have been avoiding God. Now you find yourself trailing behind in the relationship you used to have with him. Or maybe you've just never gotten close to God.

When times seem hard and problems are plaguing your life, you need the insight God can give. Go ahead; talk to him in prayer. Read a little bit of the Bible. Just run to the Lord. He understands and can help. He is waiting for you with open arms! He is there to care!

I can never be lost to your Spirit!
I can never get away from my God!
Psalm 139:7 (LB)

JUST A THOUGHT

Your heavenly Father
sends you flowers
in the springtime,
warm days in the summer,
colored leaves in the fall,
snowflakes in the winter.
Why?
Just to say, "I Love You!"

Zip Your Lip 'Bout Her New 'Do, She'll Do the Same for You!

Let's face it. Sometimes we get the urge! That wild and crazy feeling to drastically change our look, to do something new with our 'do. Maybe something short and choppy. Perhaps something edgy and totally trendy. Maybe something with super tight curls! We work up our courage, plop ourselves down in the stylist's chair, and willfully hand over our hair.

Uh, oh!

What started out as a brave attempt to live and let live, just died a sudden death. The courage that led to this folly is in a puddle on the floor!

It has happened to all of us. To me, to you, to your friends.

So tell me, when your girlfriend got the urge and went wild with her hair, how did you react when she showed her face in first period? Did you break out in hysterics telling everyone she lost her hair and her mind?

Hopefully not, because paybacks are the pits. And there will be that opportunity, because the day you get the urge, you will be in the same spot she's in!

Oh, yes, I can see it now. The hairstylist finishes her last snip and asks how you like it.

You stare in disbelief at the person who slightly resembles the person in your school photo, except for one really obvious thing: NEW HAIR!!

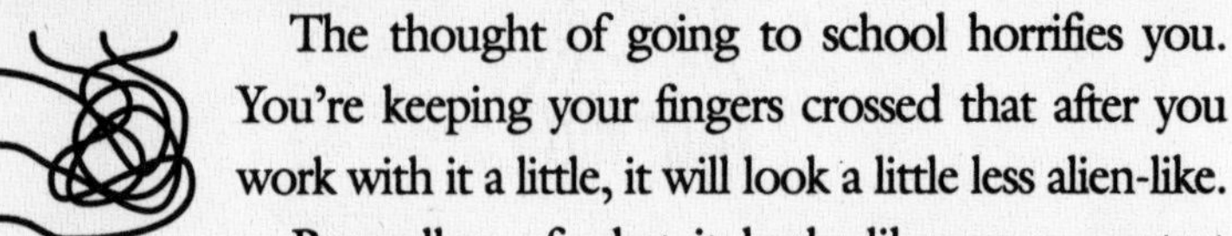

The thought of going to school horrifies you. You're keeping your fingers crossed that after you work with it a little, it will look a little less alien-like.

Regardless of what it looks like, your greatest anxiety is over "the reaction." What will your friends say? How ruthless will your brother's buddies be? And Miss "I'm so cool"? You can feel the beads of sweat forming on your forehead as you imagine that evil smile spreading across her face.

But, wait. Each of them, your friend, your bro's buds, Miss Cool, suddenly remember that when *they* showed up with their horrendous HAIRSTYLE, you were kind. Polite. No laughing. No cruel jokes.

So they get hold of themselves and give you what you gave them: *Grace!* You chose to zip your lip about their new 'do and they'll do the same for you!

Do for others what you want them to do for you.
Matthew 7:12 (LB)

Now that's some great advice for "do-do" new 'do's!

HAPPY THOUGHT

Zits are not permanent!

Samson's Bad Haircut Day ... Doomed by Delilah!

Delilah was a beautiful woman with an ugly desire for silver, about eleven hundred pieces of it! Apparently money was more important than love.

Samson loved Delilah. Yet her heart was far from his. When the lords of the Philistines offered her cash in exchange for uncovering the secret to Samson's strength, she accepted.

Delilah batted her eyes and begged Samson to tell her his secret. Enjoying the tease, Samson told her three things that were not true. Bind him with fresh cords. Bind him with new ropes. Weave his hair into seven locks. None of these were the secret to Samson's strength.

Frustrated, humiliated, and dreaming of her shopping spree at SAKS, Delilah got desperate. She used the lowest of low tactics. She issued a plea that Samson did not want to play with, for he had fallen for her, fallen hard.

She challenged his love for her by dropping her glance, pouting her lips and saying, "How can you say you love me when you don't confide in me?"

Yep. She used the ol' if-you-really-loved-me trick.

Samson fell for it! "My hair has never been cut," he confessed, "for I've been a Nazirite to God since before my birth. If my hair were cut, my strength would leave me, and I would become as weak as anyone else."

Bad move, Sammy!

Delilah lulled him to sleep with his head in her lap. She stroked his hair, then bid it goodbye as the barbers quietly came in and cut it off. His hair was gone, his strength was gone, but worse yet, the presence of the Lord was gone as well.

When the Philistines attacked, Samson awoke as a weakling. He was captured by his enemy, who gouged out his eyes and threw him into prison.

What a bad, bad, hair day!

Samson had broken his Nazirite vow by allowing his hair to be cut. (Nazirites were not to have a razor taken to their head, as their long, uncut hair was a symbol of their devotion to God.) Not only was he suffering from a broken heart (Delilah never really loved him), he was also distressed over his disobedience.

At his birth, God had called Samson to deliver the nation of Israel from the hands of the Philistines (see Judges 13). Now, here he was, blind and bound up by the very ones he was to defeat!

One day, at a drunken celebration to their god Dagon, the Philistine lords called for Samson to be hauled out of prison so they could make fun of him. But they did not realize that Samson's hair had begun to grow out and his God had forgiven him. Being placed between two pillars, Samson called out for God's help and he pushed against the pillars causing the building to fall and crushing thousands of Philistines (and himself)!

God had renewed Samson's strength. God still had Samson

fulfill the plan he had for his life. Our God is the [illegible] chances!

Like Samson, some of us might fall for the te[illegible] enemy and end up in his trap and totally off trac[illegible] when we ask God to forgive us and truly repent by changin[illegible] our ways, God restores us ... 100 percent! And what started as a bad experience can turn out to be a good one!

HAPPY THOUGHT

Bad haircuts do grow out!

~ Notable Quotable ~

PSST!

Have you heard that you are a beautiful brush stroke
in the painting of God's self-portrait?

—Pat Bigliardi

Desperate Hair Day Defenses!

Some days you're really rushed and have zippo time for your hair. Other days you've pulled out all the stops ... you've moussed, you've gelled, you've sponge rolled, but still, your hair is hopeless!

You're left with no other choice. It is time for ACTION! But don't despair. Even though you are forced to take desperate measures, you can still look absolutely adorable!

So, go ahead. Choose your defense, girl, and fight back with style!

THE BALLCAP (my personal favorite)

- Wear it forward or backward! Pull your hair through the opening in the back, or let it hang down from under the cap. Be sure all of your bangs are tucked up inside the cap.

THE VISOR

- Great for detracting from bad, bad, bangs.

THE CLAW CLIP

- Gather your hair, twist it, pull it up, and clip it.

THE MESSY MOUND

- Make a ponytail, then twist a rubber band around it, but on the last twist, pull your hair only halfway through the rubber band. Now mess it up! Make it uneven! Pull a few strands out!

THE SUNGLASSES

- Wear 'em like a headband all day!

A POINT TO PONDER

The other day my husband asked me, "Did you know your bangs come straight down, then turn straight out to the side? "Yes," I replied. Then I walked away, leaving him with a bewildered look on his face. HA! If your friends laugh at your new 'do, laugh with them. And do your 'do that way anyway!

HAPPY THOUGHT

Braces are really jewelry for your teeth.

~ Notable Quotable ~

It's so important to remember what God values most, and what he wants our lives to look like. Life isn't about cool shoes or being a great athlete. It's about who we are in Christ and what we've done to bring people to him.

—Jaci Velasquez, Recording Artist

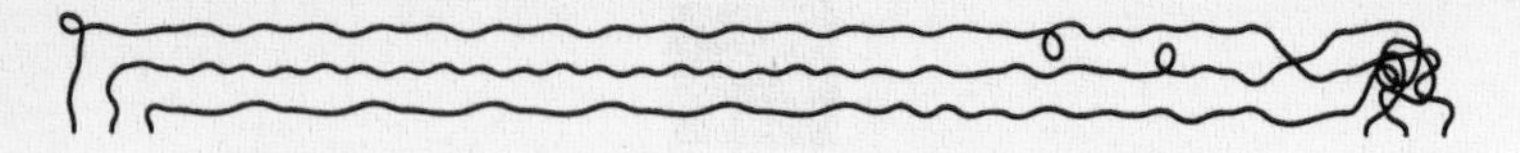

You Know It's Going to Be a BAD Hair Day When ...

...You wake up and try to brush your frizz down but it won't go away! Finally you decide your hair's going to be its own person today!

...You're too rushed for a shower and the oil in your hair has already made your color a shade darker!

...You wake up and your **cat** *is laughing at you!*

...You look into the mirror only to discover that what used to be your hair now best resembles an electrocuted porcupine that's never heard of the theory of gravity!

...You're so sleepy in the shower that you apply conditioner instead of shampoo!

...Your short, curly hair sticks up like little horns!

...You accidentally spritz your perfect 'do with water instead of hairspray!

...The red dye you used on your hair turned it orange!

~ Notable Quotable ~

The joy that shines through from having a love relationship with Christ is what makes a person truly beautiful.

—Kim Boyce, Recording Artist

Happy Stuff to Do: Just God and You!

- Write your favorite Scriptures on slips of paper, fold them up, and place them in a jar. When you need an encouraging word, open the jar and pull one out.

- Light some scented candles to create a soothing atmosphere, then slip into a hot bubble bath. Pray or read a cool Christian novel!

- Keep a Memory Box. Collect mementos, photos, love letters, notes, postcards, and programs that make you feel special. Thank God for each one!

- Sit in a special place and write a letter to God in your journal.

- Buy a special gift from God to you (I usually buy an angel to add to my collection).

- Ride in the car with the windows down and your music way up. Sing at the top of your lungs. Sing praises to the Lord!

- Before you close your eyes for the night, thank God for three things—big or little—for which you are grateful.

- Buy yourself a colorful bouquet of your favorite flowers. Every time you see them, remind yourself that they are from someone special. You!

~ Notable Quotable ~

Life is either a daring adventure or nothing at all!

—Helen Keller

Strong Is Beautiful!

A lot of popular songs talk about getting tough on the inside in order to make it through a nasty breakup. Oh, girlfriend, they have it all wrong. Believe me, putting a wall of defense around your heart does not make you strong; it makes you hard. There is a difference! It takes more than being strong to become a woman of strength. It takes the touch of the Holy Spirit and a heart yielded to God, a heart without walls.

Here's a piece a friend E-mailed to me. Give it some thought. Let these words encourage you to be a woman of true strength.

Strong or Strength

A strong woman works out every day to keep her body in shape ... but a woman of strength kneels in prayer to keep her soul in shape.

A strong woman isn't afraid of anything ... but a woman of strength shows courage in the midst of her fear.

A strong woman won't let anyone get the best of her ... but a woman of strength gives the best of herself to everyone.

A strong woman makes mistakes and avoids the same in the future ... a woman of strength realizes life's mistakes can also be God's blessings and capitalizes on them.

A strong woman walks sure-footed ... but a woman of strength knows God will catch her when she falls.

A strong woman wears the look of confidence on her face ... but a woman of strength wears grace.

A strong woman has faith that she is strong enough for the journey ... but a woman of strength has faith that it is in the journey that she will become strong.

Shared via E-mail

Which woman do you want to be?

Oh, Forget It! God Has!

We all mess up. We all do bad stuff. But because we are in God's family, we have a Dad that forgets the bad!

It's true. God forgets. And so must you.

Yes, you need to first confess it to him, and receive his forgiveness, but then you need to pack it up and ship it out!

The Scriptures say, "He remembers our sin no more!" It doesn't always work that completely with us. We will often keep beating ourselves up for something we have already been forgiven for. And the enemy—the baddest dude of all—will try to throw our mistakes in our face to keep us feeling like guilty girls, loser ladies. Well, don't let him! Whether Satan is badgering you or you keep blaming yourself, it is time to forget what God has forgiven.

Take some advice from the apostle Paul. (Remember that he used to go around persecuting and killing Christians, but God forgave him for THAT!) *"No, dear brothers, I am still not all I should be but I am bringing all my energies to bear on this one thing: Forgetting the past and looking forward to what lies ahead."* (Philippians 3:13, LB)

Forget the past and press on toward your bright future—hand in hand with a God who has forgotten!

HAPPY THOUGHT

Gummy bears are fat-free!

~ Notable Quotable ~

In the weaving of our lives, the Lord uses the dark threads of hard times to complement the colorful threads of good times. Together they create a brilliant design that otherwise would not be possible!

—Dr. Bill Stephens

~ Section Two ~

HAPPY THOUGHTS FOR FICKLE FRIENDSHIP DAYS!

Love forgets mistakes;

nagging about them

parts the best of friends.

Proverbs 17:9 (*LB*)

You Have a Forever Friend

Friends are an important part of our lives. God did not design us to be loners. He built within each of us the desire to be linked up with others.

Yet, friends can be fickle. Sometimes they're moody and we are not sure how to handle them. Sometimes their teasing goes too far and truly does hurt. Sometimes they suddenly turn competitive—acting smug about their A+, their new Gap outfit, or their invitation to the prom. Sometimes they say they want to go for pizza, then at the last minute demand Taco Bell! Sometimes they make plans with you then ditch you for a better offer. Ooh! Sometimes they leak out your private business just to have some juicy gossip to share with the clique. Ouch! That is not only being fickle, that's being unfaithful. That is the kind of friendship that might cause you to say, "Hasta la vista, baby!"

Yet there is one friend you will never have to say that to! He is a forever friend. He is a faithful friend. He is God.

Check this out!

Know therefore that the Lord your God is God;
he is the faithful God.
Deuteronomy 7:9 (NIV)

Wait, that's not all!

If we are faithless, he will remain faithful,
for he cannot disown himself.
2 Timothy 2:13 (NIV)

Get it? Because of the fact that it is part of his nature to be faithful, it is not even possible for God to be unfaithful! Or fickle!

He is a true friend, a faithful friend, and a forever friend! He will not change his mind or go back on his Word! You can trust him and depend on him! He keeps your confidences and even offers you the ultimate advice! He will never tease you or deceive you—honesty is his policy! He will never leave you, let you down, or let you feel lonely!

He truly is your forever friend.

I will not forget you! See, I have engraved you on the palms of my hands.
Isaiah 49:15-16 (NIV)

HAPPY THOUGHT

If God had a photo album,
your photo would be in it!
If God had a friendship bracelet,
he'd give it to you!
If God could live anywhere,
he'd still choose your heart!

Adapted from E-mail

So, Exactly Whatz a Friend?

FRIEND \ 'frend \ technically speaking ...

~ A person attached to another by affection or esteem; a favored companion; one who shows support.
SYNONYMS \ also known as ... Sidekick, confidant, soul mate, bosom buddy, chum, comrade, helper, rescuer.

For instance, a friend is someone who ...

- Respects you, has earned your respect, and keeps confidences.
- Makes you feel valuable and protects the friendship you share.
- Loves you and uses things, instead of loving things and using you!
- Sympathizes with you and always takes your side—yet, privately tells you when you are wrong.
- Doesn't laugh when your hair looks hilarious!
- Understands when you became so involved in your homework that you forgot to call her back!
- Willingly and humbly apologizes when she is wrong.
- Realizes people are not perfect and forgives you when you mess up!

~ Notable Quotable ~

Many people will walk in and out of your life,
but only true friends will leave footprints in your heart.

—Eleanor Roosevelt,
former First Lady of the United States

JUST A THOUGHT

A best friend is someone with whom you can do anything or nothing, and still have a great time.

You Can Become True Blue!

Are you a true-blue friend? You know, the kind others can count on? Share secrets with? Make them feel free to be themselves? Trust to be truthful? Take this quiz to figure out where you are with this whole friendship thing!

Instructions and Scoring: Read through each question, then award yourself points based on which answer best describes you!

Be honest—it is the best way to become true blue.

0 points	Nada! No way!
1 point	On rare occasions!
2 points	Making an honest effort!
3 points	Almost a sure thing!
4 points	Yes! You betcha!

Here we go:

_____ If your friend shares a deep dark secret with you, do you keep it to yourself?

_____ If you promise to help your friend with her calculus exam, but then you are invited to the movies by a guy you've been crushing on, do you keep your word?

_____ If your friend is having trouble, do you pray for her or share Scripture with her?

_____ If others put your friend down, do you defend her?

_____ If your friend does something embarrassing, do you stick by her?

_____ If your friend asks your opinion, do you tell her the truth?

_____ If your friend was supposed to meet you in the cafeteria but doesn't show, do you forgive her?

_____ If your friend is pouring out her heart, do you listen without interrupting or lecturing?

_____ If you and your friend have had a misunderstanding, do you keep talking it out until you have resolved it?

_____ If your friend keeps forgetting to return your CD, are you patient with her?

Add up your score to see how you rate as a true-blue friend!

______ Total Score

31 – 40 points	You are a terrific friend! Way to go, girlfriend! You are true-blue!
21 – 30 points	You are on the right track! Keep it up!
11 – 20 points	You have true potential!
0 – 10 points	Uh, oh! You are struggling, huh? Get some help learning to be a better friend. Pray, asking God to show you how to become a better friend, then re-read the quiz questions and evaluate the areas on which you need to work. You can even ask a trusted adult to help you with this. He or she will love it!

A POINT TO PONDER

Good friends are like wedgies! They really know your deepest self, they are intimately close, and it feels fantastic when you pick out a great one!

JUST A THOUGHT

Friends love at ALL times, even when THEY are fickle, even when YOU are fickle!

~ and ~

The best way to have friends is to be friendly.

See Proverbs 17:17 (NASB) and Proverbs 18:24 (KJV).

The World's Greatest Encourager!

You can become best friends with the World's Greatest Encourager. It's true. You can. And he really is the best, the greatest, the ultimate encourager.

OK, you know I am referring to God, right?

Well, it's true. The Bible even calls him the God of encouragement and perseverance (see Romans 15:5). He knows the perfect way to encourage you so you can keep on keeping on! See, he knows what you need before you even ask him. He knows what it will take to meet your inner longings!

How does he know that?

Because he's God. He knows everything and because he *is* God, he alone is *capable* of satisfying your deepest needs, snapping you out of your mood, easing your pain, and putting your broken heart back together again.

Wow. What a guy! What a GOD!

So, how do you go about becoming best friends with him?

Simple.

All it takes is a prayer.

Something like this: "*Dear God, I've heard about you and I know some stuff about you, but I never really considered having you as a friend. Yet I see that I need and want a relationship with you. I choose, right know, to open my heart to you. Please come in. Wash me clean from my past mistakes and mixed-up priorities. Thank you that you are who you are and that you can truly be my best friend. Help me to get to know you better! I'm so thankful that you already know all about me. Well, that's the end of my prayer, I'll talk to you again soon ... friend! Love, Me."*

Easy, huh? But that's just the beginning. Develop your friendship with God like you would any other friend! Spend time with him! Talk to him! Read his Word like a secret love letter written especially to you.

And know, deep in your heart of hearts that God is the best encourager of all because he always knows what you need. Go to him. He's waiting!

JUST A THOUGHT

Friends are angels who lift us to our feet
when our wings have trouble remembering how to fly.
Shared by E-mail

Your Hair Is Your Friend Once Again!

Just washed your hair and can't do a thing with it? Not anymore! Here are some tips to help tame your tresses and manage your mane. They will help you achieve the look you are after and cut down on your frustration level.

Cream Rinse

Detangle your hair with ease! Use a cream rinse. It makes combing wet hair easier. If you have normal, healthy hair, a cream rinse is all you need. Rinse thoroughly.

Conditioner

Go for conditioner if your hair needs some shine, some moisture, and some body. Conditioners fill in the cuticle or snags in your hair and make it stronger. Choose a lightweight or a leave-in spray type to avoid the "greasies" you can get from a thick creamy conditioner.

Mousse

This lightweight puff of foam in your palm can be used on wet or dry hair. It adds volume and lift to your hair.

Gel

About a quarter-size drop of this thick liquid can add fullness and styling stay-power to your hair. Work it through your hair with your fingers—from root to tip. Spray gel is great for that wet look!

Anti-Frizz

Moisture causes hair to frizz. That is why frizz-fighting products contain silicone—they seal the cuticle so that moisture cannot enter the hair shaft. Use as directed.

Spritz

For hard to hold or stubborn hairstyles, use a spritz for extra control. Spritz adds body and texture, but not much hold once you comb or brush through it.

Hairspray

This very essential product has a memory! Yep, it helps hair to remember how it was styled—even after you brush it out. Choose a flexible hold in a fine mist to avoid a stiff, unnatural appearance.

Perms and Waves

Give your hair a little extra pizzazz with a perm or body wave. Both use a chemical solution that restructures your hair shaft into an "S" shape, thus giving it curl. The amount of curl you get depends on the size of rod you use. The larger the rod, the larger and looser the curl. These are best done in a salon—it helps reduce the backfire possibility!

Relaxers

Hair relaxers or straighteners do just the opposite of the perm or wave—they take the natural "S" shape *out* of your hair. Be aware that when you use chemicals on your hair, it usually does some sort of damage—too dry, too frizzy, too something! Extra conditioners are usually needed.

HAPPY HINT

People who really love you don't care
what your hair looks like!

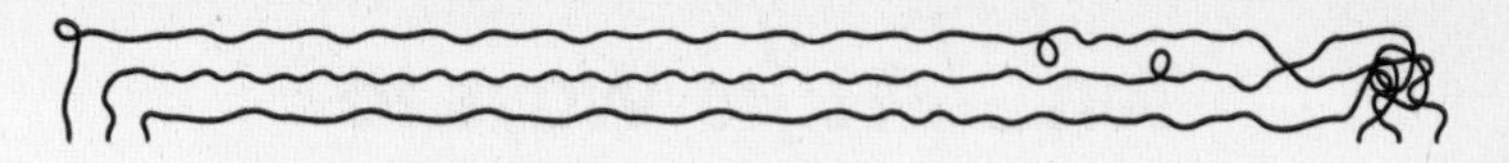

You Know It's Going to Be a BAD Hair Day When ...

...You're shopping with your girlfriends and they leave you in the dressing room talking your head off to absolutely no one!

...You give in to jealousy and backstab a friend!

...You have a poppy seed caught in your teeth but your friend doesn't tell you!

...Your closest friend just broke a promise!

...Your best friend, who is giving you a perm, unwraps the rollers and can't stop laughing!

JUST A THOUGHT

When it comes to guys, use these teen years to develop strong friendships with them, not romantic relationships. After all, great marriages are built on great friendships!

Ten *Terrific* Ways to Build Better Friendships!

1. **Make friendship a priority!**
   Some friendships happen by accident, but most are developed with effort. Be committed to putting in the needed time to plant, water, and grow lasting friendships. And *be* friendly—it's the best way to have friends.

2. **Open your eyes!**
   Friends can come from anywhere—youth group, choirs, next door, chemistry class, even unexpected places! Be on the lookout for new pals wherever you are.

3. **Show an interest in others!**
   Girls who are self-focused have very few friends. Get interested in what interests others. People love to tell you about themselves. Ask lots of questions!

4. **Break out of your age group!**
   Discover the wisdom and advice of an older woman or enjoy that fun-loving flexibility of someone younger. Your best buddies do not have to be exactly the same age as you.

5. **Get involved!**
   It's pretty tough to meet people if you hide yourself in your house, you know, hanging out in your room with your

headphones on! Get out and get involved. Volunteer at a hospital or homeless shelter, or take on a job at church—like being the youth group greeter or part of the visitation team that goes out to meet the visitors. You could always join a club, get on a committee, or run for an office! You'll gain valuable experiences and new friends!

6. **E-njoy E-xcellent E-mail!**
   Technology has made it easy to keep in touch! E-mail, chat rooms, and instant messaging are quick and simple ways to tell a friend hello or give them a lengthy play-by-play of your big shopping trip. Just remember, E-mail is OK, but there is nothing like hearing your friend's laughter and giving her an encouraging hug.

7. **Take a second look!**
   Beware of writing people off too quickly. First impressions are not always accurate. Perhaps the person is having a bad day. Give them another chance before you pass judgment and check them off your list.

8. **Set realistic expectations!**
   If you are looking for (or trying to *be*) the perfect friend—forget it! It is unrealistic to think anyone is capable of always being there for you or tuned into your needs. Likewise, you cannot do that 100 percent for someone else. Still, having some chums is better than going the loner route. Just be sure you leave room for them to be imperfectly human!

9. **Listen up!**

   Really listening to the other person shows you are interested in them and that you care! You will prove you are listening when you use what she has just said to ask another question or when you make a statement related to what was said. Also, "listen" to her body language and tone of voice.

10. **Be yourself!**

    Forget trying to be what you think others want you to be! Be genuine. Be authentic. Yes, allowing others to see the real you can be risky, but it is a risk worth taking. It is the way to true friendship.

~ Notable Quotable ~

Weak friends will teach you how to hang out.
Strong friends will teach you how to hang on!

—Richard Roberts

Mrs. Lot's Lousy Hair Day ... Faulty Friendship Turned Salty

The Bible never gives us her name, yet she is very well known. She is Lot's wife. See, you know about her, don't you? She is the one who turned into a big block of—well, let's back up.

When Lot went separate ways from his Uncle Abraham, he decided to make his home in the city of Sodom. It was a city known for its immorality and corruption. Lot became very involved with the city and was often seen at the city gate—an indication that Lot had become a man of status. Which in turn means that his wife was part of the high society scene in Sodom.

We can just picture her life there: the parties, the teas, the finest carriage, the silk garments, and the red carpet treatment—she loved it all!

She especially loved her friends. Every day they would "do lunch," if for no other reason than to be seen in public and to be admired by the peasants. She loved to bark orders to her servants so others could hear. It made her feel so important.

Mrs. Lot lived for her friends. Oh, sure, they were not perfect according to the standards of the God of Abraham, but she wanted and needed their acceptance. Yes, she had indulged in many of their sinful ways, her life was far from godly, but she reasoned within herself that being part of the "in" group was better than being obedient to some God who was "out" there.

Oops! That is where she was wrong.

I'll bet if we could ask her today, she would tell us she would have done things a little bit differently.

See, God decided to destroy the people of Sodom because of their evil, wicked ways. But first he sent two angels to get Lot and his family out of the city so they could be spared. They came to Lot and urged him to take his family and flee!

Panic struck the heart of Lot's wife.

Flee the city? As in, leave? Just walk *away* from her exciting life and her best friends? Her mind was racing. She knew of the graciousness of God, but she refused to believe he had a better plan for her life.

The angel of the Lord grabbed her hand and rushed her outside of the city. "Flee for your lives," the command came again, but with a new instruction: "And don't look back" (see Genesis 19:17).

As she ran with her family, the thought of leaving her life in Sodom pulled at her heart. As they neared a place of safety, she could hear behind her the thunderous fire falling over the city like rain. She could smell the smoke of her former life going up in flames.

Then she did the unthinkable.

She stopped. She turned. She looked back. Bad move.

Bad choice. Bad day! Actually, having already been entangled in sin, disobeying the orders of the Lord one more time wasn't so hard. But this time the results were fatal.

She turned into a tall block of solid sodium chloride! A pillar of salt. She longed for Sodom and it cost Mrs. Lot her life. What a lousy way to go!

How About You?

As a Christian, that is what happens when you get in with the wrong crowd. They pull in one direction while God pulls in another. Eventually, you'll have to make a decision.

All of us need friends. No arguing with that. But when we hang with girls who are not striving to live a life that pleases the Lord—we are headed for trouble.

Do you let your friends drag you down? Do you let them hold you back? Do you desire their acceptance over God's? Is their friendship more important to you than a friendship with God?

If so, *flee*, my friend! Run for the hills and don't look back!

Yes, pulling apart can be painful. But trust me, God has a better plan! The Lord will bring new friends—godly gals—into your life. Just ask him. He desires for you to build bonds of friendship with girls who will lift you up, not drag you down. Girls who will help you be strong when faced with temptation. Girls who will grab your hand and help you run in a direction that is pleasing to him!

~ Notable Quotable ~

The greatest love is shown when a person lays down his life for his friends; and you are my friends if you obey me. I no longer call you slaves, for a master doesn't confide in his slaves; now you are my friends, proved by the fact that I have told you everything the Father told me.

—Jesus
John 15:13-15 (LB)

Tick, Tick, Tick, KABOOM!

Six to eight preteen girls file into my living room each time I offer THE BEGINNING BEAUTY CLASS here in my home. I have had the pleasure of teaching these classes for years. I truly enjoy working with these girls on poise, manners, fitness, skin care, and personal grooming.

Recently, Annie and Teresa, who were best friends, signed up for class. They had been buddies since second grade and loved doing all the same stuff; even their mannerisms mirrored each other. But there was one thing about them that was definitely different—their bodies.

During the third week of class we were chatting about our bodies and how they change as we go through the Big P! Puberty. The more we talked, the more I noticed Teresa withdrawing from our chat.

After class I pulled her aside to do a little detective work. I wanted to know the meaning of her body language. I wanted to investigate the feelings behind those slumped shoulders and downcast eyes.

Just a few questions and I got my answer. (That detective thing was a breeze!)

Teresa was very real with her feelings. She was struggling with jealousy. See, her body had started developing last year, but Annie's body was doing nothing. Nada. Not a thing! Hence, Teresa felt like she was getting big next to Annie's petite frame.

In an effort to keep from gaining weight or having to buy the next size jeans, Teresa had started to skip meals. She was willing to go hungry in hopes of not looking larger than life compared to Annie.

How About You?

Girls, can we chat? Yes, just you and me.

When you use your friend's body (or abilities) to measure your own worth, you are on the wrong track!

See, God installed a time clock within each of our systems that is ticking along at a special rate. Who set it? God! That time clock can affect not only our bodies, but also the development of our talents and gifts, our athletic coordination, and our academic abilities—lots of things!

Why let petty jealousy affect a perfectly happy friendship? Why ruin a good thing?

Be open to what God is doing in your life and what he is doing in the lives of your friends. It may not be the same thing at the same time. But it should never keep you from being friends!

~ Notable Quotable ~

Never weigh yourself every day. A woman's weight can fluctuate by three or four pounds during the month due to water retention and hormone changes. Don't get wrapped up in weight! It's not worth it! Life's too short!

—Denise Austin, Fitness Expert

A POINT TO PONDER

Pay attention to what you are doing to shape your LIFE, not just your body!

The Best Friend Braid

Here's a hairstyle that is all about friendship! First, it requires the help of a friend. Second, it only divides hair into two strands—one for you plus one for your friend makes two!

OK, let's get started.

Comb your friend's hair straight back. Then parting her hair from her forehead back, pick up two sections of hair at the top of her head. Cross them right over left. Now add a small amount of hair from the head to each section. Cross them right over left. Now add a small amount of hair from the left side, above her ear, and add it to the section of hair you are holding on the right side. Repeat on the opposite side. Cross the two sections of hair again. Repeat these two steps until you reach the nape of her neck. Or, to continue the braid, take a small amount of hair from underneath one section, bring it around and over, and add it to the opposite section. When you reach the end of her hair, secure it with a clip, then tug on the braid to even out the tension. Add a ribbon.

HAPPY THOUGHT

Technically, popcorn counts as a vegetable!

A POINT TO PONDER

There is absolutely, 100 percent, no way, that every person you meet will become your friend. And that's perfectly normal. God makes us all different. Some people we click with, some we don't.

JUST A THOUGHT

In a weird sort of way, good friends are like good bras! They are hard to find, supportive no matter what, comfortable to be with, and always close to one's heart! Friends make great bosom buddies!

Happy Stuff to Do With Your Friends

The friendships you develop with your gal pals will be some of the deepest and richest relationships of your life. Here are some fun ideas of things you can do together to help you make great memories with great friends!

- Perfect the art of giving by surprising a teacher, Sunday school teacher, or youth director with fresh-baked cookies or a homemade card you created together!
- On a dreary, drizzly day, open up a big umbrella and go for a walk. Enjoy the rain, jump in puddles, chat about your favorite things!
- For a whole week, refuse to talk about your weight or what you've eaten!
- Rent your all-time fave flick—then act out your favorite scene. Videotape it for lifelong laughs!
- Finger paint!
- Give each other a manicure, then paint your toes with polka dots!
- Have an au natural spa night! First, drop some chamomile tea bags into a pan of super hot water, bring the water to a boil, and then remove the pan from the stove. Use a towel to make a tent over your head and, keeping a safe distance away, let the steam rise up on your faces for two to four minutes. Pat skin dry. Then whip two egg whites with a blender until stiff. Add three drops of lemon juice. Apply to

your face for ten to fifteen minutes for a refreshing, protein plus mask! Rinse with warm water. Breathe deeply and relax! Slide on some aloe vera gel or Vitamin E cream as a moisturizer for a finishing touch!

- Collect travel magazines, vacation brochures, and AAA tour books, and plan your dream vacation! Include location, what to pack, activities to do, and whom you would take with you.
- Choose a sports team and become fanatical fans!
- Sign up for dancing lessons. Learn how to salsa, swing, tango, or twist! Or try a self-defense class. What fun!
- Design a Web page together.
- Put on a puppet show for the neighborhood kids—make it about Jesus (lots of parables to choose from)—then tell the kids how much he loves them.
- Befriend a new or lonely girl; draw her into your circle of friends.

HAPPY HINT

Numb skin with an ice cube before plucking hairy eyebrows! Get a friend to help!

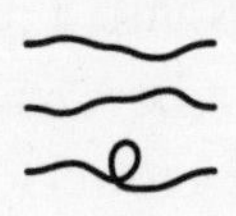

~ Section Three ~

HAPPY THOUGHTS FOR SUPER MOODY DAYS!

Cast all your cares and worries on the Lord!

He absolutely cares for you!

(See 1 Peter 5:7)

The Choice to Rejoice!

One of the happiest verses in the Bible reminds us, "This is the day the Lord has made; let us rejoice and be glad in it" (Psalm 118:24, NIV). How's that for an awesome thought!

Why not make it personal …

This is the day that the Lord has made,

I will rejoice and be glad in it!

Just for fun, let's emphasize different words in each phrase. Say them out loud, putting some punch behind the bold word.

THIS** is the day! This **IS** the day! This is the **DAY!
*Yes, this is the day that the **LORD** has made!*
*I will! I **WILL!** I will? Yes, I **WILL!***
*I will **REJOICE** and be glad in it!*
*I will rejoice and be **GLAD** in it!*

No matter which word you emphasize, the point is clear: *To rejoice is a choice!* Yes, indeed. It is up to you and me to make a choice about how we will enter our day. Will we choose to be grateful or grumpy? Optimistic or pessimistic? Glad or sad?

When we make the choice to rejoice, we can't help but be glad! Our joyous attitude will affect the way we look at life—all day long!

One day at a time, maybe one hour at a time, *choose to rejoice.* You will be glad you did!

Yes, I will bless the Lord and not forget the glorious things he does for me!
Psalm 103:2 (LB)

~ Notable Quotable ~

Optimism is the cheerful frame of mind that enables a teakettle to sing, though in hot water up to its nose!

—Anonymous

HAPPY THOUGHT

Moods are like seasons. They will eventually change!

Moody? Whatz That?

MOOD \ 'müd \ technically speaking …

- ~ a conscious state of mind
- ~ predominant emotion; a feeling
- ~ a prevailing attitude or disposition.

SYNONYMS \ also known as …

Attitude, tendency, vent, inclination, craving, appetite, feeling, outlook, frame of mind.

MOODY \ 'müd-é\

- ~ expression of a mood (usually associated with being gloomy)
- ~ temperamental (as in impulsively changing from one mood to another)

SYNONYMS \ also known as …

Gloomy, unhappy, down in the dumps, out of sorts, cheerless, heavy-hearted, sulky, melancholy, wavering, cantankerous, wounded, hurt, irritable, snappy, huffy, testy.

JUST A THOUGHT

When life gives you lemons, make lemonade ... or lemonade pops! Just blend lemon juice, water, and sugar together to create the taste you love, then pour into plastic molds or small paper cups. Freeze! (Add sticks after 1 1/2 hours.) They will sweeten your mood!

Murky Mood? Walk It Off!

You can do a very simple thing that will help you shake off any mood that is threatening to squeeze the joy right out of your day.

All you need is a decent pair of walking shoes and you'll be ready.

Walking is the easiest, most effective way I know of to change your mood (well, besides prayer, of course!) Just today, I felt a little overwhelmed, sort of like life was closing in on me. So, I laced up my New Balance 801's® and headed out the door.

It was truly an incredible thirty minutes.

I spotted a patch of vibrant orange poppies ... a horse walked over to his fence to greet me ... the sun on my shoulders felt like a warm hug ... I kicked a pebble and it reminded me that "skipping" was fun, so I skipped!

Little by little, the cares of the world started to slip off my shoulders. Panic turned to peaceful.

So head out on a walk and watch how an "internal" bad hair day can turn into a good one!

Walking Do's!

- The first few minutes, concentrate on taking deep, cleansing breaths in and out!

- Pop up a quick prayer, asking the Lord to meet you on this walk and come along with you!

- Be observant with every step! Don't just see what is around you, really *look* at it!

- Listen to the sounds around you. Birds, rustling leaves, the scampering of squirrels, whistle of the wind, whatever!

- Pick up the pace for at least fifteen minutes. A brisk walk will increase your oxygen, which energizes your body and your brain. It also releases endorphins into your bloodstream—your body's natural mood elevators! Enjoy!

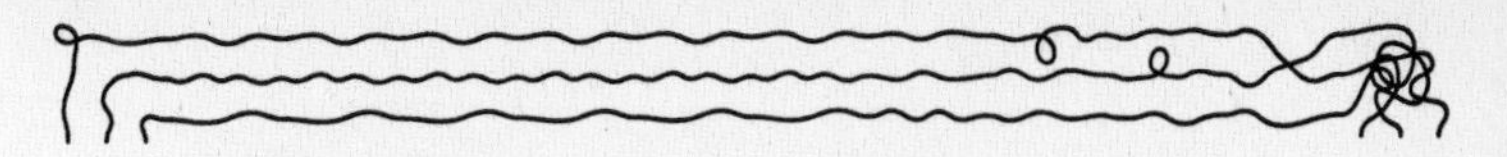

You Know It's Going to Be a BAD Hair Day When ...

... the first thing you see when you open your eyes in the morning is an overcast sky! Humidity is tough on hair!

... from the moment you wake up, everything you touch breaks, everything you pick up falls, and everything you need gets lost! Ugh!

... you started your period and you're feeling grumpy and irritable!

... you wake up and just don't feel like yourself— you don't know who *you feel like—but it's not you!*

... your stomach is in knots over something really important that you have to do.

... you tossed and turned all night and now your hair looks like a salad!

Big Sis Insight: Pamper That Pout!

I've always been a sensitive person. One who thinks and feels very deeply. It seems I often wind up feeling discontent. Discouragement frequently knocks on my door, and unfortunately I let it in. I end up being grouchy and pouty. Not a pretty picture!

My point is that it's not unusual for me to be down or in a bad mood. I have learned that it is important for me to do what I can to change my disposition. I have to open the door back up and politely invite discontentment and discouragement to leave!

I am not one to push myself in an effort to snap out of my mood. I prefer to pamper my way to a prettier mood! I do that by fixing myself up on the outside. I spend a little extra time on my hair and makeup. I use a shimmery eye shadow, add a touch of shiny gloss to my lips, paint my nails, and then I give myself a spritz of fragrance—Clinique's "Happy" is my favorite (even the name reminds me of my goal!).

I don't stop there! I choose to wear a special outfit, one that makes me feel elegant or fancy, fun or cozy, or just plain confident.

When I pamper myself on the outside, I start to feel better

on the inside. The discouragement lifts, the discontentment fades. Pampering my way to a prettier mood might sound a little goofy, but it works for me! And I believe it will work for you!

—Karen, 23

~ Notable Quotable ~

Keep a list of blessings in your life.
Go over the list each morning and remember that you have reason to celebrate every day!

—Emily Barnes

HAPPY THOUGHT

This too shall pass!

Naomi's Un-Pleasant Hair Day ... Bitter Gets Better!

The name Naomi means "pleasant," yet *this* Naomi definitely had cause to be unpleasant. The past several years of her life had been tough. For instance, there was the food shortage—the big famine that drove Naomi and her husband to the land of Moab in search of a better life for their family.

Before long, Naomi's husband died. She found herself in a foreign land with two boys to raise. When they grew up, they each married a Moabite girl. They all bonded together to build a life for themselves. Naomi loved being with her sons and their wives Orpah and Ruth. They were dear to her, as she was to them.

Yet life had another loss in store. Naomi's two sons died. Grief struck her heart once again. Feeling very alone, she decided to send her sons' wives back to their families and return to her hometown of Bethlehem.

The young women clung to her, they hugged, and they cried. Though Orpah went home, Ruth refused to go. She loved Naomi and was obviously concerned about her. She had watched her once pleasant mother-in-law become an unpleasant person to be around. Naomi had allowed her losses to build resentment in her heart. She felt abandoned and alone. She was no longer her pleasant self. She had become bitter.

Ruth refused to leave her. She just knew that with hope, love, and the Lord, Naomi could get back to being her normal self.

Together they traveled back to Bethlehem, where Naomi announced, upon her arrival, "Don't call me Naomi. Call me Mara." See, Mara means "bitter." It sounds unpleasant, and that's what Naomi had become. Her outlook was bleak, her attitude was negative, and her disposition was pessimistic.

Thank goodness for Ruth!

Little did "Mara" know what a blessing her daughter-in-law would be. Yes, Ruth had lost her husband. Yes, she was the one who had now moved to a foreign land. Yet, she was the one who was optimistic about life. She was sure that Naomi's God (the God she was learning to love) would care for them.

Ruth came up with a plan. She would go and glean in a field for free grain. They would not starve. They could survive!

Her positive outlook led her right to the fields of the kind and wealthy Boaz. Turns out he was a relative of Naomi's. He not only favored Ruth, giving her protection and ordering his workers to purposely drop grain for her to pick up, but he was taken with her disposition.

She was bright. Hard working. Courageous. Optimistic.

Boaz couldn't hide his feelings for long.

He fell for Ruth and they married!

Wow! Look what optimism reaped: grain, wedding gifts, and a great husband! And not just for Ruth. "Mara" was part of the plan, too. She was now going to be well cared for.

Slowly, "Mara" realized that God had not forgotten her. He had not abandoned her. He had not stopped loving her. Slowly, the bitterness, pessimism, and negative outlook faded. Naomi became pleasant once again.

Have you ever let emotions get the best of you? Do you let life draw you into being pessimistic or optimistic? Are you a negative or positive thinker?

Naomi and Ruth were in the same situation, yet they reacted completely differently. Naomi made life more difficult, Ruth made it more desirable! Be an optimistic, positive kind of gal! It makes life more fun!

Note: Like Ruth, if you have a person in your life who seems negative most of the time, don't give up on her! Perhaps your encouragement and love can help her through this tough time and get her back to her "pleasant" self.

HAPPY THOUGHT

God's mercies are new every morning!

JUST A THOUGHT

The Lord will make known to you the path of life,
the plan he has drafted just for you.
It is a plan for good and not for evil.
In his presence you will find fullness of joy.
Yes, when you keep him in the midst of every day
and you do what he asks,
then your joy will be overflowing.
In his right hand there are pleasures forever
that he offers to you.

—Adapted from Psalm 16:11, Jeremiah 29:11, and John 15:5, 11

Girl Talk

What do you do to turn negative thoughts into positive ones? Here's advice from fellow teens:

- I take one step at a time toward a better attitude—it seems easier that way.
- I think of all the possible outcomes of my situation. Then I focus on the positive ones!
- Pray! Pray! Pray!
- I talk it out with my mom.
- I think about how I could handle the situation next time, and try to learn from it.
- I keep in mind that all things have a purpose and God is working everything out according to his plan.
- I call my best friend. She always cheers me up and gets me laughing! Then I can think more positively!
- I look at old pictures and take a trip down memory lane! It always gives me a sense of hope to know that I've *had* happy times and *will* have more in the future—even if I'm in a funk right now!
- I start by asking God to help me be willing to *be willing* to have a positive thought about the person or circumstance that has got me down.
- I eat chocolate!
- I keep in mind that everything in this life is temporary! The best is yet to come!
- I get in God's Word; get his perspective! He is great at changing my stinkin' thinkin'!

Your turn! Brainstorm three ways that you can turn gnarly, negative thoughts into peppy, positive ones!

____

____

____

____

____

____

____

____

____

____

____

____

HAPPY HINT

Don't sweat the small stuff, and remember that it is *all* small stuff!

Dance It Away!

David did it! Miriam did it! I do it!

I'm talking about dancing before the Lord. A praise or worshipful dance. Praise dancing is energetic—with clapping hands and waving arms and maybe a leap or two! Worshipful dance may be slower, more flowing as you get focused on the Lord, as you lift your arms as an expression of love and thanksgiving.

It feels odd at first. Actually moving from side to side, flowing with the rhythm of the music, lifting your hands as you twirl around the room. Yet once you get past the initial awkwardness, there is something remarkable that happens, if you let it. As you dance before the Lord, the Holy Spirit becomes your partner. As you follow his lead, he replaces your feelings of heaviness with a garment of praise. He gives you joy when all you had was sorrow. He turns your mourning into dancing (see Psalm 30:11, Isaiah 61:1-3).

Though David, Miriam, and the children of Israel danced and rejoiced out in the open, I prefer to do mine privately. I make sure no one will walk in on me. I want to feel completely free to get lost in the praise, to dance, to kneel, to laugh, to cry, to be loud, to be quiet, to pray. Then I choose music that is truly **praise** music—sometimes with words, sometimes just instrumental.

As you begin, ask the Lord to be with you, to speak to you, to show you why you feel the way you do, and to help you give it to him. Then let the dancing begin. And feel the heaviness end! It is only there, in God's presence, that we can get what we truly need to satisfy our inner needs, to heal our hurting emotions, to lift our spirits and let them soar! There, in his presence, he will give you a reason to dance. Go with it!

Check out these dancing scriptures!

Exodus 15:20-21; 2 Samuel 6:14-16; Psalm 150:3; Ecclesiastes 3:4

Try praise CD's by these artists to put you in the groove!

Petra Praise; Sonic Flood; Passion; Hillsong Youth

HAPPY THOUGHT

There is no danger of developing eyestrain from looking on the bright side of things!

A POINT TO PONDER

Negative emotions are not a sin, they are a sign. They are trying to get your attention to tell you something in your life is out of whack. Something's wrong. Something needs to be fixed, healed, resolved, or removed! Is there something your emotions are trying to tell you today?

HAPPY HINT

There is a good side to tough times! These times teach us to turn to God, to be sensitive and comforting to others, to develop our faith, to evaluate our lives, and to recognize our need for God. And that's good!

Nine Knock-Out Ways to Pump Up Your Spirit!

When you're in the dumps or you've got the grouchies, try a few of these tips. They can lift your spirits and add sparkle to your life!

- Treat yourself like a hotel guest! Just before bedtime, go in and turn down the comforter and sheets. Then place a candy on your pillow. Spritz your sheets with your favorite scent. Sweet dreams!
- Put your Bible, devotional book, pen, and prayer journal in a pretty basket. Carry it with you to a cozy spot to spend time with the Lord.
- Share your musical or acting talent with a local rest home or children's hospital. Brightening someone else's mood will definitely brighten yours!
- Re-read one of your favorite childhood fairy tales.
- Write notes to those who are important in your life. Tell them just that! Make the notes fancy with stickers, rubber stamps, or gel pens.
- Read brief autobiographies of missionaries. They are always an inspiration.
- Rearrange your bedroom. Paint the walls an upbeat color! Toss some bright new throw pillows on your bed.
- Decorate a card with your favorite Scripture verse on it. Then place it where you'll see it every day—inside your locker, on your closet door, or next to your sink.
- Call a friend and share your prayer needs over the phone. Then pray!

Bloom Where You Are Planted

I love to take photographs.

Occasionally, I will have to park along the side of the road, and hoof it into nature to get the exact shot I have conjured up in my mind.

One day I was taking pictures of these cool-looking cows. I had to walk quite a ways into the field to get a super close-up shot. As I was looking at my surroundings through my camera lens, I saw an amazing sight!

Way out in the middle of this dry, dusty field was a tiny patch of wildflowers. Though their surroundings looked bleak, they were blooming right where God had planted them!

I have received letters from lots of girls who are so unhappy. One girl's family had just moved across the country; another girl had moved across town.

One girl's parents had split up and she was being tossed back and forth between houses and schools. Life was a constant balancing act.

I can't leave out the fifteen-year-old who had been diagnosed with juvenile diabetes. The disease was trying to control her life and she was allowing her anger to eat her up on the inside.

Need I go on?

How About You?

In case you haven't noticed, life is not perfect. We often get plopped down in places we never expected to be! Things are not as we had hoped!

But take a lesson from the wildflowers.

No matter how dry, destitute, disastrous, and downright ugly your life seems, it is possible for you to bloom where you are planted. You can do more than survive, my friend, you can thrive! You *can* make the most of your situation and refuse to allow the dry, dusty ground around you determine your disposition.

First, trust that God is in control and he has planted you exactly where he wants you to be. It may not look positive, but remember, God is omniscient! He knows exactly what he is doing.

Second, sink your roots deep into the soil of God's Word. Let it be the nourishment you need to germinate, sprout, and flourish in your situation.

Third, water yourself daily with prayer—long prayers, or pop-up prayers. Ask the Lord to open your heart to the possibilities and the positive aspects of being right where you are. Remember, if your heart is not into it, you will not bloom!

Refuse to believe the lie that the grass is always greener on the other side of the fence!

JUST A THOUGHT

When you're super moody, don't fight it out, write it out!
Let your thoughts and feelings out in a journal.

Hair Blues!

Does your hair have the blues? Is it not responding the way it normally does? What's up?

Maybe you are using the wrong shampoo for your hair type or too much conditioner! Poor eating habits might be the culprit! Remember, you are not just satisfying your taste buds when you eat, you are feeding your entire body. Your hair is nourished through the blood circulating in your scalp. An unbalanced diet leaves your hair dull and lifeless. Inward care of your hair is as important as outward care.

Hormonal changes during your menstrual cycle can affect your skin, but did you know hormones can make your hair temperamental, too? The effect varies, depending on our hair and body chemistry. Dryness, oiliness, less curl, tighter curl, or total limpness are all possible reactions. Stress can also be reflected in the condition of your hair. Drastically changing hair response or loss of hair can be stress related. Yep, when you wig-out, so does your hair!

You can see that your hair, even though it has no feeling, can be directly affected by what goes on in your body. So eat well, sleep well, relax well, and your hair is bound to have a better day!

HAPPY THOUGHT

Flexible people don't get bent out of shape!

~ Notable Quotable ~

Keep your face to the sunshine and you cannot see the shadows.

—Helen Keller

No Mess-ing with PMS-ing

When you've got a major case of PMS, it is not a good time for you to mess with others, or for them to mess with you!

PMS, premenstrual syndrome, is that "oh so special" time right before your period when you may feel irritable, icky, crabby, depressed, mopey, or dopey! If you're like most girls, you will either have bloating (fluid retention), aching, breast tenderness, mood swings, headaches, fatigue, weight gain, anxiety, or cramps. Or any combination thereof! PMS symptoms may be mild or severe, depending on your body or the month.

Why does all this messy stuff occur?

Well, it has to do with hormone changes and the way your body reacts to them. In the first two weeks of the average twenty-eight-day cycle, your estrogen levels are on the rise. Then your follicle-stimulating hormone gets in on the action as it works to ripen one egg in your ovaries. When that egg is ripe, your body releases yet another hormone called luteinizing hormone. Its job is to release the egg into the fallopian tube. Then your estrogen level decreases and your progesterone slips into gear! This hormone prepares the lining of your uterus to receive a fertilized egg.

When there is no fertilized egg that implants into the uterus, the progesterone level drops and the lining is shed—thus, you get your period!

No wonder you can feel so lousy—there's a lot of stuff going on!

Tips to Make You Feel Better

During PMS (before your flow begins), pamper yourself with a warm bath, a cup of mint tea, a bedtime novel, or whatever comforts you. Get plenty of exercise, drink lots of water, eat super healthy foods, and take vitamins and calcium.

Once your period starts, treat cramps with a heating pad, hot water bottle, or ibuprofen.

Take it easy, avoid overloading your schedule, don't hang with your friends if all you can do is complain, don't make any major decisions, cry whenever you want! Be aware that you may be oversensitive during this time, so don't take people's remarks too seriously or the wrong way.

And most important of all, remember that it's just a matter of time before things will return to normal. For a while anyway!

Note: To those of you who breeze through your periods with hardly any of these symptoms, please be patient with those who do have them!
Suggestion: For severe PMS, consult your doctor about pain medication, diuretics, or anti-anxiety medications.

Sleep Your Way out of a Slump!

Could a lack of zzz's be responsible for your "grumpies?" Could your late nights and early mornings leave you feeling slow-mo' and kinda' low?

Take this quiz to find out if you are getting enough sleep.

Do you:	**YES**	**NO**
A. Get easily frustrated during the day?	___	___
B. Detest the idea of exercise?	___	___
C. Stay up late reading or watching TV?	___	___
D. Depend on a double latte to jump-start your morning?	___	___
E. Hear the teacher but have no clue what he's talking about?	___	___

If your YES column is full, it is time to make sleep a priority!

Research proves that most teens are not getting enough sleep. The average amount of zzz's needed per night is ... nine hours!

No, I'm not kidding!

God designed our bodies to require sleep. Sleep allows us to rest and recharge. It helps our bodies stay balanced. It helps to keep our moods level.

Lack of sleep can cause irritability, fatigue, lack of concentration, snappiness, stress, and the blues.

Who needs that?

Not you! So, what do you do?

Glad you asked!

Here are some hints to help you sleep better!

- Set regular sleep hours and stick to them! You will function best if you are on a schedule. Try 9:00 P.M. to 6:00 A.M. A routine will let your body know it's snoozing-time!
- Organize yourself! Actually *do* homework during study hall! Finish what's left before dinner. The later you wait, the *longer* it may take you, since your brain and body are running out of fuel!
- Exercise regularly! Just don't exercise right before bedtime or it might be too hard for your body to slow down. Consistent exercise will help you sleep and give you a general feeling of well-being during the day.
- Cut caffeine! This stimulant gives you a false sense of energy and can totally interrupt your sleep pattern. So, forget the coffee, colas, teas, and chocolate late in the day.
- Sweets can steal your sweetness! Sugar highs from candy, cakes, cookies, and sodas can cause you to toss all night and turn out grumpy.
- Do something relaxing. Before bed, take a warm bath, drink chamomile tea, listen to soothing music, read your Bible, write in your journal. Let your mind

melt away its cares and concerns and calmly float off to sleep. *"When you lie down, your sleep will be sweet"* (Proverbs 3:24 NIV).

JUST A THOUGHT

If you are ever feeling lonesome or blue,
think of me up here thinking of you!
Love, Your heavenly Father

Big Sis Insight: The Big "D"

My parents fought for as long as I could remember. There was continuous tension in our home. No one was ever sure who would be in what kind of mood. Especially if my dad had a rough day at work—anything could send him into a rage.

During my sophomore year in high school, my parents finally split up. It was such a hard and cold time for me. I was truly torn up—not just on the outside, but also on the inside. Logically, I knew I was not to blame, but emotionally I felt like I could have done something to keep them together.

As time went on, being shifted from Mom's to Dad's, from Dad's to Mom's, I started getting really, really sad. I did not know it then, but now I know I was quite depressed.

Depression can come on slowly from a prolonged situation or quite quickly from a sudden thing—like divorce, moving, getting fired, or losing a loved one. Either way, a person ends up feeling swallowed up!

At least I did. I started withdrawing from my friends. Going out just wasn't fun anymore. I also seemed to lose interest in my artwork and my keyboard—two things I used to love doing. Physically, I was drained most of the time and would stay in bed whenever possible. I can barely believe it now, but I also lost my appetite! Not even pizza or Oreos sounded good anymore, especially when my stomach hurt.

Sounds like I was a mess, huh? Well, I have learned that everything I felt were common symptoms of depression. It wasn't until my grades started slipping that someone took notice of me and I got help. My school guidance counselor set me up with a therapist who was a wonderful Christian woman.

She introduced me to something that really helped turn me around. It is called self-talk!

Whether we want to admit it or not, we all talk to ourselves. We all have thoughts and comments roaming through our minds most of the time. Those thoughts really do affect the way we feel.

Even the Bible says, "As [a man] thinketh in his heart, so is he" (Proverbs 23:7, KJV). What we *choose* to think and believe will affect our behavior.

I learned to listen to what I was saying and to change it. I caught myself saying things like, "I should drop out of life, I'm no good at anything, no one really likes me, I've got a loser family, I am so ugly, I'm dumb—I can't even pass a little quiz—and on and on!" Sometimes my thoughts got really scary.

But as I stopped those thoughts midstream, I would change them. "I can do this, I am a good person, I can try harder and pass next time, I have beautiful eyes and naturally great fingernails, every family has problems, and I am a valuable person."

Positive self-talk is the key that unlocked my depression. I started feeling alive again and my perspective on life got much better. Even today I pay attention to what I say to myself and how I say it. I know I am a precious daughter of the King of kings, and I am loved and valued by my heavenly Father. He wants me to be filled with joy, not depression.

He wants the same for you.

—Debbie, 22

Biblically Sound Self-Talk

These totally true, absolutely accurate, Scripture-based statements are guaranteed to boost your mood!

- † *I can do all things through Christ who gives me strength.*
- † *I am acceptable to God.*
- † *I am not perfect, but I am forgiven.*
- † *I have the mind of Christ.*
- † *I am never separated from God's love.*
- † *I am fearfully and wonderfully made.*
- † *I am loved and I am lovable.*
- † *I am a work in progress. God is not finished with me yet.*
- † *My adequacy is from God.*
- † *I find my joy in the Lord and it gives me strength throughout the day.*
- † *God is working all things together for my good and his glory.*
- † *God has a plan and purpose for my life—a plan for good and not for evil.*

Use these statements to talk yourself into a merry mood!

~ Notable Quotable ~

The Lord is close to the brokenhearted and saves those who are crushed in spirit.
A righteous man may have many troubles, but the Lord delivers him from them all.

—King David, Psalm 34:18–19 (NIV)

HAPPY HINT

On super moody days, try not to make any major decisions about anything! Tomorrow you may see it from a completely different perspective!

ANOTHER HAPPY HINT!

Don't feed your fickle emotions with food! When you're mad—forgive! When you're sad—talk it out with someone! When you're glad—treat yourself to something other than a batch of cookies or a whole bag of chips!

Bring Light to a Dark Mood

Have you just had it? Can't take it anymore? Feel like life is closing in? If feelings of despair and hopelessness threaten to darken your soul, it is time to force open the shutters of your heart and let some light in! The scripture teaches that God is light and in him there is no darkness. God's Kingdom is the Kingdom of Light! (see John 8:12, Colossians 1:13).

So, if God is light, who is the author of darkness? Yes, the enemy himself, Satan. His goal is to keep our thoughts in darkness and squeeze all the joy and happiness out of our life. How does he do it? He lies to us. If he can get us to believe his lies, it will keep us locked in his dungeon of darkness.

What kind of lies? This kind: No one cares about you! You are beyond hope! Your situation can't change. You have no one to turn to. Everyone hates you. Your parents don't love you, don't trust you, and don't want you. Your friends think you're stupid, a loser. There's no God whom you can trust. There's no God who loves you. There's no God with the answers. There is no God.

These are lies. All of them.

Refuse to believe them.

Stop these fiery darts of the enemy.

Fight him off by opening your heart to LIGHT himself! That's Jesus!

See, if you are already a Christian, but have gone to a place of dark thoughts with dark moods, it indicates that you have fallen for the lies and have forgotten about the light. Go back to the light. It will crush the darkness. Resist Satan and he will flee! Then start praising Jesus! Satan hates that. As you praise the Lord and draw near to him, the Bible promises God will draw near to you.

Put up your shield of faith and attack the enemy with the TRUTH, with God's Word!

That is exactly how Jesus fought Satan off—he quoted the truth of Scripture to him. Check it out in Matthew 4:1-11. Note verse 11. The devil left Jesus and the angels came to minister to him!

Refuse to believe the enemy's lies! Force yourself to get into the light, the truth, the Word! Don't depend on your own strength. Call in the backup troops! Be brave and ask a mature Christian adult for help. Refuse to stay in the darkness alone. Let someone take your hand and lead you to the truth, and walk you into the light.

You are worth it.

You are loved and cared about.

You do have a mighty, living God who is reaching his hand out to you.

Please. Take it!

A POINT TO PONDER

If you have a small view of God,
your problems will look BIG!
If you have a big view of God,
your problems will look small.

Little Lifters for **BIG** *Letdowns*

If you are a part of a family, it is bound to happen. If you have friends, it is bound to happen. If you interact with anyone on any level, it is bound to happen. If you are alive and breathing this very second, it is bound to happen!

BIG LETDOWNS! They are bound to happen!! Any of these sound familiar?

Cindy was crushed when her mom blabbed in front of her friends that she had bled on the sheets when she had started her period last night.

Misty had worked so hard on her "Celebrate History" project. She couldn't believe she wasn't selected as a presenter! How could her project be passed by?

Brittnee was squelched when Greg retracted his invitation to the Winter Formal and asked Catherine instead.

Erin had prayed earnestly for weeks for God to show her how to handle Krista's constant lying. She was out of patience—and still no news from heaven!

Potentially, there are a "bazillion" things that could let you down and leave you feeling disappointed and discouraged! The list is endless!

Fact is, letdowns happen!

Time for a Change!

Here are a few ways to lift yourself up when you are down in the dumps.

- Read through the Psalms. You'll be able to identify with many of David's feelings of discouragement. But take note. God comes through every time and David's thoughts turn to praise!
- Let go of your *shoulds*. If things don't go the way you think they should or people didn't do what you think they should have, you *will* be set up for letdowns. Having a long list of "what should have happened" will leave you knotted up inside.
- Get a different viewpoint. Take a step back and look at the situation from a broader perspective. Will life go on? Yes! Can you survive? You bet!
- Forgive mistakes and go on! You mess up and so do others. You are not responsible for them, only for yourself. Your reaction is the only thing you can control. So, let it go and love them anyway!
- Beware of becoming lost in "if only." You can dig yourself deeper into despair if you let your thoughts run amuck with "if only!" If only she ... if only he ... if only I ... if only God ... STOP! "If only" cannot change the facts of what has happened. When it comes to "if only," DON'T GO THERE!

JUST A THOUGHT

May life give you just enough clouds
to create a beautiful sunset!

"Tear-iffic!"

I love a good cry.

There is just nothing like a big bawl, a serious sob session, and a total washout! Controlled tears are OK, too, but the real cleansing comes from a good, hard cry.

Really. Let it rip! If you are afraid of being heard, sob into a pillow or go into your closet. Just give yourself permission and do it.

Crying is a "tear-iffic" emotional release. It's like you're forcing all the stress, anger, frustration, and sadness out through those tears. Of course, people cry when they are happy, too. Crying is an inner cleansing. Afterward, you'll feel drained, relaxed, tired—and ready to start again, taking life in bite-sized chunks, one piece at a time.

Be comforted in knowing that John 11:35 says that "Jesus wept."

Now that's my kind of guy!

JUST A THOUGHT

Lord, if love is all I need, then all I need is You!

"For God is love." 1 John 4:8 (NASB)

~ Section Four ~

HAPPY THOUGHTS FOR ROUGH FAMILY DAYS!

Listen to your father and mother.

What you learn from them

will stand you in good stead;

it will gain you many honors.

Proverbs 1:8-9 (LB)

Family? Great Idea!

God was very clever when he created the family. He chose to bring together a man and a woman, bond them in a spiritual covenant, and then give them a lifetime together with the goal of becoming one.

But that's not all he gave them. He gave them children! Yes, little bundles of energy that would keep them up at night and on their toes during the day. (My sister's family recently picked me up at the Richmond airport and driving back to their home, my three-year-old niece proudly announced to me, "My Daddy has nose hairs." Lingering in the air were those few brief moments of silence as I carefully weighed my response! Hooting laughter was all I could come up with! Then I graciously offered my tweezers to my brother-in-law just in case there were some strays he wanted to pluck!) Kids are so funny!

Back to God's Plan

God planned that those children would all too soon grow up to become sometimes tender, sometimes terrifying teens. They, too, would grow (and struggle) to be young adults who would eventually marry and start a new family unit. (OK, that's basically how it works.)

Here's my point. God came up with the idea of families!

A family is designed to be a place where we learn to love, to be patient, to be kind, to be aware that there are others in this world who have feelings, needs, and opinions. We learn we cannot always have our own way and misunderstandings are inevitable, but that compromise, forgiveness, and unconditional acceptance reap blessings untold.

God knew that friends would come and go, but that our family would *always* be our family! They would be there for us to laugh with, cry with, and pray with. They would be there to help us up when we fall, help us through when we're weary, help us over when we are weak.

But did God know that within families there would be conflict and struggle, anger and pain? Yes, he did. (Check out Genesis for a peek into some pretty pesky families.)

Yet in the midst of all that, I believe he longs for us to mend broken fences, to keep loving when love is not returned, and to continue reaching out even when the risk is great.

How do we do all that? We must lean on him. It is not easy being in a family. That's why God promises to supply us with the inner "stuff" we need to do what he asks. We need love? He's got plenty to fill us with. We need forgiveness? He will empower us to be able to forgive. The list goes on. We must trust him and lean on him to give us what we need to be the kind of family he has in his mind's eye.

I am pretty sure he wants us to do one more thing. It is to be thankful for our family. Can you do that? Will you?

Start today to pray for each family member, tell them you love them, encourage them, forgive them, write a note, send an E-mail, treat them to one of their "favorites." Whatever it takes, make the effort to be thankful and to let them know it! After all, they were God's idea!

JUST A THOUGHT

You can choose your friends, your classes, your clothes, and your CD's, but you can't choose your family. God does that for you. Yes, the all-wise, all-knowing God purposely chose to place you in your particular (and sometimes peculiar) family.

~ Notable Quotable ~

God grant me the serenity to accept the things I cannot change, courage to change the things I can, and wisdom to know the difference.

—Reinhold Niebuhr

Here's How to Define a Family!

FAMILY \ fam·i·.ly\ 'fam (ə) lē \ technically speaking ...

~ a group of people related by common ancestry
~ a group of individuals living under the same roof; household
~ a group of people united by certain connections and beliefs
~ a group of people bonded by love

SYNONYMS \ also known as ...

Parents and children, brood, clan, kin, relatives, descendants, offspring, siblings, brothers and sisters, bloodline.

Sandpaper Days

Your mom says you have to baby-sit your younger sister. You had plans; you don't want to do it.

You took the trash out like you were told, but your dad didn't like the way you placed the can so close to the curb and he told you about it—loudly!

Your brother purposely bumped into you, walking down the hall. You wish you could crush him.

Oh, yes. Sandpaper days.

You know, the ones that are rough. The ones where every single family member rubs you the wrong way. The ones where it is just hard to get along with anyone!

Well, don't lose heart. There is hope. Patience is the way to smooth out your sandpaper days.

Rather than mouthing off, pushing back, behaving rudely, and making matters worse, be patient.

Take a deep breath. Step back. Refuse to react to someone's irritating ways. Keep snide comments from getting under your skin. Turn inconvenience into an opportunity to be calm, to be patient. Don't complain. Don't raise your voice. Prove you can be good-natured and positive under pressure.

Patience will keep you from saying something you cannot take back, from throwing a childish tantrum, from building walls in your relationships.

Patience will take the rough rub out of your day-to-day family life!

It will also add some amazement to your household! You will be amazed at how others react to your patience, and they will be amazed that you are being patient!

Goodbye, sandpaper.

Hello, smooth patience!

Dear brothers, is your life full of difficulties and temptations? Then be happy, for when the way is rough, your patience has a chance to grow. So let it grow, and don't try to squirm out of your problems. For when your patience is finally in full bloom, then you will be ready for anything, strong in character, full and complete.

James 1:2-4 (LB)

~ Notable Quotable ~

If life were predictable, it would cease to be life and be without flavor.

—Eleanor Roosevelt,
former First Lady of the United States

Tactful "Talk Back" Tactics!

Yep. Talking keeps the communication going between you and your parents so you can get to the root of the problem. The thing is, you have to do it RIGHT!

Check out this checklist:

- ✓ Do not, I repeat, do not yell at your parents. They may be older than you, but they can hear just fine. Speak to them in a controlled, respectful tone of voice. Avoid huffing and heavy sighs!
- ✓ Face them when you are talking to them. Turning away and closing up with your body language communicates that you do not have an open mind. If you

want them to stop being narrow-minded, you need to do the same. And, oh, yeah—uncross those arms!

- ✓ Focus your eyes on theirs! This shows you are paying attention—which is a necessity. Parents get real uptight when you act like you are ignoring them.
- ✓ Walk and talk if you need to. Shoot some hoops. Go bowling. Play slap jacks—whatever! Doing an activity with your parents somehow eases the tension and makes you think more clearly.
- ✓ Truly listen. If you are planning your response while they are still talking, then you are not fully hearing what they are saying!
- ✓ Calm down if you are revved up! Getting your emotions under control, or waiting until your parents calm down, makes for better chats.
- ✓ Get their perspective. Ask questions. Gather information. Repeat to them what you understand them to be saying. Make sure you are on the same page.
- ✓ Refuse to allow hateful, poisonous words to come out of your mouth. It's not fair throwing darts at their hearts. And always tell the truth.
- ✓ Respect their position. Understand God has given them the awesome responsibility of raising you. It can be a tough job and your parents are just people! They may seem overprotective—that's because they don't want anything bad to happen to you. Believe it or not, they *do* know more than you do about the way the world works. Why buck their desire to keep you safe from the world's evil ways? Be glad they care. Some parents don't.

Big Sis Insight: Honoring Is Easy

Honor your father and your mother!

I used to cringe when I heard those words. It was just the hardest thing for me to do. To honor means to show respect. That meant I needed to obey them, listen to them, put their requests above my wishes, and be polite and loving toward them.

There were just so many times I thought I could not do it and that they did not deserve it. Then I heard my youth pastor teach on a verse I had not been aware of. It was Colossians 3:20. It says, *"Children, be obedient to your parents in all things, for this is well-pleasing to the Lord"* (*NASB*).

It was that last part that made the difference.

When I honored and obeyed my parents, I was pleasing Jesus! It really wasn't about my parents at all, it was about the Lord.

I definitely knew I wanted to please the Lord, so this made the honoring thing so much easier. Each time I would remind myself *that* was why I was honoring my parents. It wasn't because I felt like it or because I thought they deserved it! It was because of Jesus. I need to tell you though, the best part was that it greatly improved my relationship with my mom and dad. It made for a less stressful and more peaceful existence at home.

Honoring is so worth it!

—Sharon, 29

HAPPY HINT

Live one day at a time and make it a masterpiece!

But They Drive Me Crazy!

Fasten your seatbelt, it's gonna be a fast ride!

You are now going to have the incredible opportunity to write down everything about each family member that threatens to send you to the psycho ward!

Get a pen. Get a grip. (I know you're excited about this.) Get started!

Stuff that bugs me about my dad:

____

____

____

____

____

Stuff that bugs me about my mom:

____

____

____

____

____

Stuff that bugs me about my sister/brother: (List each one individually)

____

____

____

____

____

CONGRATULATIONS!

You have just successfully completed a prayer list! Yep. You are looking at a list of attitudes and behaviors about your family that you can now be praying about. Pray for each person and each item individually. Then pay attention to how God answers your prayers.

Please note that if everyone drives you equally bonkers, then perhaps the problem is not *them*. Perhaps it is you. Perhaps if you changed—lightened up, were less sensitive, lowered your expectations—life at home would be more pleasant and the stuff about everyone else that bugged you so much won't bug you at all!

Pray for them, pray for yourself.

Just pray.

HAPPY THOUGHT

An irritating sibling can grow up to be your best friend.

Hagar's Rough Family Day ... Always Running, but Never Too Far for GOD!

To say it was complicated is putting it mildly. There were Abraham, Sarah, and Hagar; Abraham and Hagar's son, Ishmael; Abraham and Sarah's son, Isaac. Hagar worked for Sarah.

It was a unique combination of his, mine, and ours! A blended family at best.

Allow me to give you a quick family overview. Abraham and Sarah were wealthy landowners who had no children. God had promised to give them a son, but as they aged, so did their faith. Then Sarah thought up the brilliant plan of giving her maidservant, Hagar, to Abraham so that Abraham would get his son through her.

The plan worked, but the joy Sarah thought she would feel backfired. (It's never a good idea to take matters into your own hands!) Hagar, however, liked the situation. She was now feeling favored and special. She was with child; Sarah wasn't.

There was contention, hatred, and jealousy between the two women.

Hagar overheard Sarah complaining to Abraham about her. But she never expected what happened next.

Sarah called her into her chambers and she beat her.

Astounded and broken, Hagar ran away. She ran fast and she ran far. When her strength was gone, her legs weak, she fell to her knees! Between sobs, she thought she heard her name.

"Hagar."

Indeed, she did.

An angel of the Lord came to her—right there in the desert—to chat with her. She explained she was running from Sarah. The Angel of the Lord instructed her to return to Sarah and act as she should! No more prideful boasting in the face of a barren Sarah!

Hagar obeyed.

She gave birth to her son, Ishmael.

But as years passed, all was not swell!

As a teen boy, Ishmael was teasing his younger half-brother, Isaac. (Yes, Abraham and Sarah finally had a son.) He liked picking on the fair-haired mama's boy. Again, Sarah got upset and went to Abraham. She demanded Hagar and Ishmael be sent away.

Reluctantly, Abraham packed food and water, then sent them away.

A Scary Situation

Hagar and Ishmael wandered aimlessly in the wilderness. When their supplies ran out, Hagar knew there was no hope, nowhere to turn, no one out there to help her.

She left Ishmael crying under the shade of a bush, then walked away from him and fell into a heap of tears. She sobbed uncontrollably as her thoughts turned more and more fearful.

How did she get in this situation? What could she do? Did she have to watch Ishmael die? How could life be so rotten and unfair again?

Even though Hagar was lost in the depths of despair, she was never out of God's reach. He sent an angel to her once again!

See, God heard her crying. He knew exactly where she was. He knew what had happened. And he came to her.

The angel of God called to her from the sky.

"Hagar."

Hagar heard her name, lifted her head and looked up.

"Hagar, what's wrong? Don't be afraid! For God has heard

the lad's cries as he is lying there. Go and get him and comfort him, for I will make a great nation from his descendants."

Then the coolest thing happened. God put a well full of water in front of her, right there in the desert! He was personally taking care of Hagar and her son. Then she cried again, but this time her tears were tears of relief! She ran to the well, filled her canteen and took it to Ishmael. With hope in her heart, and a promise from God, she knew they were going to be OK (see Genesis 16, 21).

How About You?

Has your family situation ever gotten "scary" like Hagar's? Have you had misunderstandings, hurt feelings, and brokenness? Have you had really rough family days that left you feeling dejected and alone?

God is standing next to you saying, "Do not be afraid, I hear your cries, I know what's happening and I will take care of you."

Hear him call *your* name.

Lift up your head.

Look at him.

Hear his instructions.

He will be there for you.

I promise.

Happy Stuff to Do *With Your Family*

Is it true that families that play together stay together? Turn up your family's fun factor with these ideas!

- Try a new recipe—select it, shop for it, make it, serve it!
- Go garage sale hopping! Growing up, this was one of my family's favorite Saturday morning activities. There are treasures to be found!
- Spend a rainy afternoon going through photo albums or home videos.
- While hanging out watching TV, treat each other to a peppermint cream shoulder rub or foot massage! You can find the cream at a body and bath shop or at your local drug store.
- Go to the zoo or the beach. Build the ultimate sand castle. Fly a kite. See who can get theirs the highest! Go fishing, water skiing, or picnicking!
- Create a Family Game Night. Play a game of Monopoly, Who Wants to be a Millionaire?, or Outburst. It's good, healthy competition and lots of fun!
- Find an issue you all feel strongly about, educate yourselves, and take a stand! Speak out! Get involved! Make it your family cause!

Mother's Day Memorable Moments

- Ask her to share what she and her mom liked to do when she was a teen.
- Serve her favorite dinner on the floor of the family room—picnic style.
- Get siblings together and make a video imitating all the things your mom does that you appreciate and things that make you laugh (you know, like that special mom "look").
- Give her a flower—a simple blossom can melt her heart.
- Go to the mall together and try on all kinds of unique outfits!

Father's Day Fun Tips

- Turn on some Big Band music and dance around the living room—most dads love this! (If your dad is like mine, he can even teach you how to dance!)
- Volunteer to help him with a project.
- Make a coupon book with chores your dad can cash in anytime.
- Wash the car—inside and out!
- Challenge him to a game of chess, see who can get the most strikes while bowling, shoot some hoops, or play tennis. Join him in something he likes!

"Me And Mom"

Practically every teen girl goes through it. The mom thing. Yes, the two of you used to be joined at the hip, but you're not so hip about being seen with her anymore. In fact, you are embarrassed by her clothes, her hair, her geeky comments, her—well, just HER!

And chances are, deep down, you're feeling sorta bad about it. That's a good sign! It is the girls who don't feel bad about it that I'm concerned about.

The tension between moms and daughters during the teen years can be tight. You are forging ahead to establish your personal identity and independence. Your mom is trying to let go of you, but it hurts her to see and feel you pull away. Moms struggle. Sometimes moms asks tons of questions or they gripe at you when you are not even sure why. Some moms say mean things. Some don't say anything. Most say things they don't "mean to say so mean"! They just don't know exactly how to handle wanting to hold you close *and* wanting to let you go so you can fly.

See, as you grow up, your mom feels like you don't *need* her anymore. You may have even convinced yourself that you don't.

But deep down, it's not true. You do need her. And she needs you.

Go tell her. Go climb on her bed and have a heart-to-heart with her. Ease the tension. And do something that will be good for both you *and* her ... let her hold you!

You Can Turn Bickering Into Blessings!

Sports are not really my thing, I admit it. Yet spectating is even more painful to me than playing! Especially tennis. That ball gets smacked back and forth, back and forth, back and forth. Serve and return. Serve and return. It gets old. Boring.

So does bickering. That back and forth, back and forth, petty arguing. It is like two people nipping and picking at each other. It must get old for God, listening to parents and kids, kids and kids, bicker all the time.

That's probably why he included this in the Bible:

"To sum up, let all be harmonious, sympathetic, brotherly, kindhearted, and humble in spirit; not returning evil for evil, or insult for insult, but giving a blessing instead; for you were called for the very purpose that you might inherit a blessing."

1 Peter 3:8-9 (*NASB*)

Pretty straightforward, huh?

How About You?

What can you return when your irritating little sibling serves you something evil? *Kindness.*

What about when your overworked and underpaid dad puts down your new hair style? *A humble smile.*

And when your mother insults your closest friend? *Volley back a blessing!*

Turn back and forth bickering into a game of blessings.

The final score?

Love to love!

Great Dad-Daughter Connections!

Dads can sometimes exasperate kids—you know, irritate them, annoy them, totally bug them, or embarrass them. Whether your dad pokes fun at you, calls you by the quirkiest nickname, continues to read the paper when you ask him a question, insists on screening every phone call ... don't let it get to you.

You know, sometimes dads have a weird way of showing their daughters some attention. Some of them do it any way they can, which doesn't always translate to you as warm and fuzzy. In fact, some dads are not even involved in their daughters' lives at all. Maybe your folks are divorced (50 percent of them are) and you rarely see your dad. If you hurt, you have a right to. I'm so glad you have God as your heavenly Father. In fact, he promises to be a Father to the fatherless!

Maybe your dad *is* in the picture, but your relationship is rocky. Since God tells us to honor and respect our parents, here are things you can do to improve that father-daughter connection.

- Don't give him *reason* to exasperate you! Be obedient! Be polite!
- Honor him by acknowledging his authority. Don't be sassy.
- Appreciate the fact that he goes to work every day to provide for you.
- Ask him a question or two about work, sports, or church. Get to know him!
- Pray for him. He needs God to help him be a great dad.

- Have a date night. Head out to a park, to the batting cages, or for a game of miniature golf; rake leaves together; go for ice cream. It will be worth it!

Pull the Reins on Rage!

"I'm so ticked off," Karen hissed out as she ran the dreadful scene through her mind again. "How could my brother Mark be such a jerk? How could he have the nerve to embarrass me like that? I'll get back at him. I'll make him pay. I'll—"

WAIT A MINUTE, KAREN, her conscience yelled back.

The discussion they had last week in Sunday school suddenly struck her mind like lightning. She could hear her teacher's words echoing in her mind:

"It's OK to be angry about certain things, but don't let that anger make you sin. And never go to sleep angry or still in a fight with someone. Get rid of anger quickly before you give Satan a chance to lead you into doing the wrong thing."

The message rang loud and clear, racing through Karen's mind!

There are situations in families that will cause you to be angry. Anger itself is not wrong. It is often an involuntary emotion that needs to be controlled. But beware, there is good anger and then there is bad anger. Being angry at poverty, homelessness, abortion, or social injustice is valid. This kind of anger can motivate us to take action against these situations. It is constructive anger. But bad anger, which includes most anger, tends to be negative. Jealousy over a sister's good fortune, being criticized unfairly, being stuck at home instead of at a friend's party, someone lying to you, and hurt feelings, cause the kind of anger that needs to be dealt with quickly because it leads to sin.

Just as there is good or bad anger, there are good and bad ways to handle your anger. Let's look at a few of the not-so-hot ways people deal with it.

Repressors!

Repressing angry feelings means to ignore them and not admit they are even there. Perhaps not even be *aware* they are there! This keeps the anger in the subconscious where it can lead to depression.

Suppressors!

Suppressing your anger means to hold on to it, to stuff it down, to slam the lid on it. You know it is there, but you won't deal with it. Yet eventually suppressed anger shows up in the body through headaches, stomach troubles, or breakouts. It may even show up in actions like rebellion, under- or overeating, alcohol or drug abuse.

Expressors!

Expressing anger comes out in screaming, blaming, hatred, rage, or revenge! All of these lead to explosive results. Expressors spew their anger out on others.

Do any of these sound familiar? Anyone in your family fit these descriptions? What about you?

How does the Lord want us to handle anger?

First, recognize it and nip it in the bud. How? By taking it to him. Tell him all about it, then surrender it to him.

Now, open your heart and allow him to give you the *desire* and *ability* to forgive and forget the situation that triggered the anger in the first place.

From this point on take these scriptural suggestions to heart!

† Don't have a quick temper. Be slow to anger. (see James 1:19)

† Don't allow anger to lead you into sin. (see Ephesians 4:26)

† Don't let the sun go down on your anger. Get over it quickly. (see Ephesians 4:26)

† Always speak the truth in love, never in anger! (see Ephesians 4:15)

JUST A THOUGHT

When faced with explosive fathers, nagging mothers,
oblivious brothers, oversensitive sisters, irritating
aunts and uncles, cruel cousins, or ungrateful
grandparents …
just remember that other people
have bad hair days, too!

Rough Hair Day Q & A!

Q: *My hair is extremely soft and fine. It is hard for me to put it up because it slips out. Any tips?*

A: Try applying mousse to your freshly towel-dried hair. Then blow-dry and style. If it still slips out of your up-swept 'do, try a super-thick gel. It will add a noticeable amount of volume to your hair.

Q: *Some days my hair has horrible static cling. What can I do?*

A: Keep a few of your mom's nonstatic dryer sheets in your bathroom. Very lightly, rub your hair with one. Or, try a detangling product that says it reduces static cling.

Q: *My hair has that fly-away look. What can I do to bring it back down to earth?*

A: Simply spray your brush with hairspray. Now brush through your hair as usual. No more fly-aways!

Q: *I shower daily but only wash my hair every other day. On the "no-wash" days, how can I perk it up?*

A: For medium or long hair, try this. Roll your hair—tip to root—in medium- to large-sized Velcro rollers. While you shower, the steam from the hot water will set the curls. Allow hair to air dry while you apply your makeup. Now, unroll, comb out, and style!

Q: *I like the straight sleek look, but my hair has some natural wave. How can I get it to cooperate?*

A: Wash and condition your hair with moisturizing products. Then, as you are blow-drying on a low setting, use a paddle brush to straighten your hair as you dry it.

HAPPY HINT

Where do you go when you can't fix your hair?
The hairstylist!

~ Notable Quotable ~

So where do you go when you can't fix your life?
The only place to go is back to the
One who made you.

—Sheila Walsh

Frantic Family Time: Dinner!

Is your family going in a zillion different directions? Do you have crazy schedules? Ever lose track of each other?

Dinner to the rescue!

Dinner serves as a time to connect with those other people who live in your house. Remember them? Yes, they are the ones occupying the other bedrooms, the ones who hog the bathroom mirror!

Even if you only manage to pull together two or three times a week, it will be worth it. So help gather the troops together and go for it! Take a real interest in your family's lives! Here are some ideas to get the conversation rolling.

Table Time Chatter

- Tell your family the funniest (or weirdest) thing that happened to you that day. (It will help you look for the "humor" in life). Shared laughter reminds everyone that being in the family is a fun thing. Ask others what laughable thing happened to them!
- Ask your mom or dad to explain something about work—a special project, interesting client, etc.!
- Coax each person to share the best part of his or her day.
- Encourage everyone to daydream about this year's vacation options.
- For older brothers and sisters, check in on term papers, teacher quirks, sports activities, band or choir rehearsals ... the possibilities are endless!
- Ask younger brothers or sisters what they are learning in class—ABC's, adding and subtracting, a special song. Get them to sing for you!
- Thank your mom for the meal, ask about the recipe, the ingredients, her favorite meal as a teen.
- Keep in mind that your goal is to find out what is going on in the lives of the wonderful, yet totally unique, folks in your family. You will feel more connected and have a sense of belonging when *you* help make dinnertime happen at your house!

HAPPY THOUGHT

By his mighty power that is at work within you,
God is able to do far more than you could ever ask,
think, or dream--way beyond your highest prayers,
desires, thoughts, or hopes!
(See Ephesians 3:20.)

Big Sis Insight: Family Secrets

My family had a secret.

I never told anyone, not even my best friend! I know she thought it was odd that I would rarely invite her to my house, but she never said anything. She just welcomed me at her house and included me in her family activities.

It is hard to admit the secret now, even though I've dealt with it and it is out in the open. Seeing it on paper is hard, but here goes.

My mother is an alcoholic.

I always thought my brother was the lucky one. He was much older than I and had moved out years ago, long before it got really bad.

I did my best to hide my secret and hide my pain.

I was never honest about Mom.

My friends would see my mom at school. She taught violin part-time at the high school.

It was hard enough being teased or overhearing jokes about your mom and her "fiddle," or how she was "out of tune," or "had a few strings loose." Students always joked about teachers, but this was my mom.

I could only imagine what they would say if they knew what she was like when we got home. Mom wasn't a raging, angry drunk, she was the type that goes into a stupor then falls asleep. She would sleep through dinner, the dishes, the laundry, the housecleaning, and the shopping. My dad was away at work as often as possible, so I picked up the pieces to help us appear like a normal, functioning family.

I was carrying such a heavy burden. Now I know it would have been better, been "healthier" for me if I would have shared my secret. My best friend was a Christian and I know she would have prayed with me and for me. Plus, other kids had alcoholic parents, too. I could have used their support.

It is counterproductive to work so hard at covering up a family secret. Now I feel a freedom from the bondage of it all. I understand I was not to blame, and I was not responsible for my mom's actions. She needed help. I needed help. And as long as I was silent, that help did not come.

May I ask if you also have a family secret? Is it alcohol related? Drug related? Have you or a sibling been verbally abused? Sexually abused? Has someone in your family had an abortion? Is anyone struggling with an eating disorder?

I encourage you to get honest, then get help. You are not alone. There are people and organizations that want to help. Trust me.

—Julie, 34

HAPPY THOUGHT

For nothing is impossible with God.

Luke 1:37 (NIV)

Special Sister, Special Friend

You always see their names together in the Bible. Mary and Martha. Martha and Mary. Neither ever married or had kids (that we know of). They used their time to serve the Lord, and while Jesus was on earth, they had a special calling to care for him. Nonetheless, they could get on each other's nerves. My favorite example is when Martha wanted help fixing a meal and got mad at Mary for not helping. She even tried to get Jesus to make Mary get in the kitchen and get busy! Ha! Yes, though they were practically inseparable, they still had their spats.

So did my sisters and I ... Allison, one-and-a-half years older, Alisa, three-and-a-half years younger. Allison and I shared a room for seventeen years. We had those typical "stay on your own side of the room" disputes. Alisa and I would get into knockdown drag-outs. I specifically recall a really intense hair-pulling session. (My dad had to break that one up!)

Sisters can seem like a major source of annoyance, but Martha would have never traded Mary for anyone else. I would have never traded Allison or Alisa, either.

I believe God places a special bond between sisters. It is there if we let ourselves feel it. They are given to us to share that secret knowing of the inner workings of our hearts. Because they live with us day in and day out, they have the potential to see us at our best and at our worst. And they still love us! We still love them!

Develop a friendship with your sister(s). Be there for her. She'll be there for you. It's a precious relationship.

Brainless Brothers, or Not!

You've questioned it many times, but let me assure you, there ***is*** something inside of your brother's brain!

Hard to believe, huh?

See, God made boys so differently than he made girls. That makes it more difficult for sisters to understand their brothers ... because they are boys! They're guys!

Take this little quiz to see how clued-in you are about those differences!

True/False

A. _____ _____ Guys want to hear all the flowery details of your day.

B. _____ _____ Emotionally, guys are sensitive, like delicate butterflies.

C. _____ _____ Guys are more production-oriented than relationship-oriented.

D. _____ _____ Mentally, guys are very good at focusing on lots of things at one time.

E. _____ _____ Guys and girls are physiologically the same.

Let's see how you did!

A is FALSE!

Most guys, most brothers, will just want to hear the basic facts. They are logical thinkers and don't need to analyze stuff like girls do.

B is FALSE!

Generally speaking, a guy's sensitivity more accurately resembles a buffalo, not a butterfly! They are thicker-skinned and don't take life so personally.

C is TRUE!

Girls tend to be more interested in people than opinions. Your brother is more production focused. Got a problem? He'll just fix it and be done with it.

D is FALSE!

Guys are best at focusing on one thing at a time.

E is FALSE!

Guys' chemistry, chromosomes, and hormones are different than girls'. That explains a lot of stuff!

God definitely designed brothers and sisters to be different!

I encourage you not to take their actions and reactions so personally. When they do something weird, just remember—they're guys! Go figure! Love 'em anyway!

Perfect Moments

It was a moment I will never forget.

On the stage of the Miss Oklahoma Pageant in front of thousands of people, I had just finished performing an instrumental piece on my classical guitar. The auditorium exploded with applause. I drew a deep breath and smiled.

It was a perfect moment.

Did I win the pageant? No. (Second runner-up.) Did I win the talent competition? No. (Swimsuit!) In fact, the rest of the pageant wasn't so phenomenal! Come to think of it, the whole week had become a comedy of errors. Yet tucked inside, there was one perfect moment.

Realistically, that is the way life is. There are no perfect days, perfect weeks, perfect years, perfect vacations, perfect tournaments, perfect families, perfect youth groups, perfect friends, perfect jobs, perfect haircuts, perfect anything!

And Yet ...

Where do we get the notion that everything is supposed to be perfect? Maybe from TV. That's where we see the problem laid out, looked at, and solved in thirty minutes or less! Or maybe from novels and fairy tales, where the author had the opportunity to *write* the perfect ending.

Unfortunately, that's not real life. That's not the real deal. Life is full of good and bad, ups and downs. Lots of mediocre. Lots of ordinary. Lots of reality.

Yet, they are there. The perfect moments.

Look for them.

They'll make you smile.

The Babe Seminar!

God thinks you're a BABE! Andrea will prove it in this fun, upbeat seminar designed especially for teen girls. Listen while Andrea chats with you about:

Learning to LOVE Your Look!

Sensational Skin & Model Style Make-up!

How to Be Unbelievably Beautiful From the Inside Out!

For more information about The BABE Seminar contact:

Andrea Stephens
P.O. Box 2856
Bakersfield, California 93303

Or check out her website at:
www.andreastephens.com

It's a great idea for your youth outreach event, retreat, camp, or luncheon at your church or school!